The Real Self
Love Handbook

A Proven 5-Step Process to Liberate Your Authentic Self, Build Resilience and Live an Epic Life

Andrea Pennington, MD, C. Ac.

Founder of the Real Self Love Movement

Foreword by Karena Virginia

MAKE YOUR MARK GLOBAL

MAKE YOUR MARK GLOBAL PUBLISHING, LTD
USA & Monaco
The Real Self Love Handbook © 2019 Andrea Pennington, MD, C. Ac.
Published by Make Your Mark Global Publishing, LTD

Book cover design: Andrea Danon & Stefan Komljenović of Art Biro Network www.artbiro.ba
Cover photo Copyright 2019 In Her Image Photography www.InHerImagePhoto.com

Library of Congress Cataloging-in-Publication Data
Library of Congress Control Number: 2017917382
The Real Self Love Handbook
Publisher: Make Your Mark Global, LTD
Fernley, Nevada
p.336
Trade Paperback ISBN 978-0-9994949-8-1
Hardcover ISBN 978-1-7341526-0-9
Ebook ISBN 978-0-9994949-5-0

Subjects: Psychology
Summary: As a functional depressive, Dr. Andrea Pennington enjoyed a high powered media career with all the outer appearances of success. But she was miserable inside. After years of battling 'Imposter Syndrome' and constantly striving for perfection, a spiritual awakening prompted her to break free and live as her Authentic Self. After more than a decade of research and experience with her patients, a 5-step self-discovery framework emerged called The Cornerstone Process. The Real Self Love Handbook outlines this process and includes the latest research from positive psychology, neuroscience, mindfulness meditation, energy psychology, compassion practices and life planning.

MAKE YOUR MARK GLOBAL PUBLISHING, LTD
USA
The Real Self Love Handbook © 2019 *Andrea Pennington*
For information on bulk purchase orders of this book or to book Dr. Andrea to speak at your event or on your program, call +33 06 12 74 77 09 or send an email to Booking@AndreaPennington.com

Praise for *The Real Self Love Handbook*

"With a level of vulnerability and authenticity that is both refreshing and rare, Dr. Andrea shares a beautiful story of listening to one's own heart. A must-read for anyone on spiritual and purpose-driven paths."

— Mike Dow, Psy.D., Ph.D.
NY Times bestselling author, Heal Your Drained Brain
www.DrMikeDow.com

"Self-love is not a cure in the same sense as a pill or a detox. Rather it is our original factory setting to be restored. I'm delighted that a fellow physician is addressing this in the public eye, giving more weight to what we have known deep down for years. Health and happiness starts from within."

— Mark Hyman,
MD #1 New York Times Bestselling Author of
Food: What the Heck Should I Eat?
and Director, Cleveland Clinic Center for Functional Medicine

"If you ever felt the concept of 'real self love' sounded sweet but a tad selfish, read this book. If you ever felt trapped in a vicious cycle of negative life situations and negative moods, read this book. Not only is Dr Andrea a formidable story teller sharing relatable life lessons openly and helpfully, she is also a medical professional who has studied both western medical modalities as well as eastern traditions. The result of her 'life well-lived' is a brilliant handbook that brings the full power of 'self-love' to the forefront for anyone eager to improve

their life in all ways. Far from a selfish pursuit, 'real self-love'
promises to be the answer to unlock the full potential of who we are."

— Bruce Cryer, Former CEO, HeartMath,
Co-author, From Chaos to Coherence:
The Power to Change Performance, Founder,
Renaissance Human, Adjunct faculty, Stanford University

"Before even reading this book, I literally wrote to Andrea asking 'Have you ever experienced total bliss, then completely had the worst low ever?' I didn't realize those were some of her EXACT words in her own story. This book is absolutely incredible....it feels as if she climbed inside of my body, mind, and soul, and IS me.

I feel Andrea opens up the conversation to people to truly be seen and heard and acknowledged to a degree that they've never felt before but always desired, and that each and every person that reads this will have that same experience I had....a literal "take your breath away" feeling of finally being understood, and not alone. It is truly amazing and an honor to witness her vulnerability."

— Dr. "Juicy" Jill Stocker
Co-author, *Time to Rise*
www.JillStocker.com

"In this beautiful book is an amazing manual for a greater life of well-being. Dr. Andrea delivers the strong message of Love and addresses the urgency and responsibility for us as individuals to take better care of ourselves. Once you have adapted these simple steps that Andrea offers towards self-love, the effect will not only change your life but also affect the people around you and will spiral onwards to your

whole community. Her deep wisdom and insights shine through the entire book and leave you inspired to make a difference in this world starting with your own transformation.

I am grateful that we have such strong, empowering individuals like Andrea who is willing to share her whole story, with no parts left out, were we get to mirror ourselves also in the vulnerable sides of it and get at the same time get the right tools to grow from it.

From the bottom of my heart I encourage you to become the best version of yourself and adapt Andrea's 5 Cornerstones of Real Self-love."

— Sólveig Þórarinsdóttir
Yogi, Author, Founder of Solir Yoga Studio and #LoveWarrior
www.LoveWarrior.is

"What an amazing gift this book is for everyone who will be reading it. No matter how far you are on your journey of inner work, fulfilling your purpose and making difference in the world I am confident this book will give you new insights and inspiration as well as practical down to earth guidance and healing. Reading the book it I could feel Dr Andrea talking to me, sharing her amazing journey with me to guide me on my journey as well. The book carries the richness, the depth, the width of knowledge as well the joy, playfulness and child-like openness and wondering that Andrea embodies. And she is very much spot on: Before we want to serve others and the world we need to discover, live and love who we truly are."

— Bea Benkova, Founder and CEO of
The Global Institute for Extraordinary Women

"If you've been on your path to letting go of stress, anxiety and depression be sure you read this. It is the end of your search. The answers lie in these pages.

It is so rare to read such an inspiring book. No matter who you are these feelings can affect us all. The love, dedication and true passion for transformation that Andrea shares is seen in every inch of this book. It gives me goosebumps just to read it!"

— Yvette Taylor
Creator of The Energy Alignment Method
Transformational Mentor Speaker & Author
www.EnergyAlignmentMethod.com

"Dr. Andrea Pennington has once again written from the heart on what matters most—being our authentic selves--as we commit ourselves to "be the change we wish to see in the world." In "The Real Self Love Handbook," Dr. Andrea Pennington brings real-life moments to the page illustrating how to overcome the darkest of times, including depression, anger, and self-loathing, bringing joy and light into life's issues and challenges. Pennington awakens a heightened sense of empowerment and understanding that we can be uplifted out of darkness and into the light of our true authentic selves."

— Missy Crutchfield
Co-Founder and Editor-in-Chief of Gandhi's Be Magazine
www.BeMagazine.org

"You want to know who your Authentic Self is? "A Writer must write, Painter must paint, Dancer must dance..." In this book are practical ways to help you through your journey to your Authentic Self. Dr. Andrea shows us through her vulnerability and courage how *we can learn self-love, self-compassion, and to take responsibility for our precious Life. Encouraging, inspiring, and Life-Changing!!"*

— Trevor Hahn
Advocate for The National Suicide Prevention Line
Hotline: 1-800-273-8255
www.RescueMeAsap.org

"After doing the hard, but well-needed work to say "I Love You, Me!", Dr. Andrea Pennington is more than qualified and capable to empower men and women to learn, accept, live, and love their original self. I can say this because her writing has delivered me into the sole purpose of living my true identity. This book is strategically put together to walk you through step-by-step the process of releasing "the imposter you" and living as the real you.

It is my prayer and hope that as you read this greatly needed book you will discover the essence of your identity and be response-able to cultivate, nurture, and appreciate the true authentic you."

— Dr. Janet L. Anthony
Co-author, *Time to Rise*

"Andrea Pennington's heart and dedication shine through every page and make the love she writes about very real to us as her readers. This profound yet practical book is showing an actual path to the true love that we've all been missing. And then a way to create the life that we will love as well!"

— Halina Goldstein
Spiritual mentor, speaker, teacher at HalinaGold.com and
Founder of the Joy Keepers Network

"I believe some of us are here to experience, to learn and to bring a message to the world that sometimes, just sometimes, science alone does not hold every answer. Sometimes there's a middle ground between that which we can explain and the 'other' - Andrea might call it the 'woo woo factor', I might (to positively reclaim a phrase once use disparagingly) call #HippyShit.

'The Real Self Love Handbook' carries plenty of practical exercises to satisfy the brain, lots of spirituality and faith to satisfy the heart and enough soul-deep, personal anecdotes from Andrea to take the reader by the hand and guide them through a safe, trusted and life-changing journey of positive transformation.

By giving so much of herself in this book, Dr. Andrea Pennington has made it entirely possible for readers to trust, let go and emerge with a new sense of self, purpose and clarity.

A power-full book of beauty, truth and possibilities.

Thank you, Andrea, for all that you bring to the world - not least with this book."

—Taz Thornton, inspirational speaker, best selling author
Founder of the #UnleashYourAwesome personal
development movement & #BrandMastery Programme
www.TazThornton.com

"I resonated with 'The Real Self Love Handbook' on so many levels... We often hear how important it is to 'love yourself' and put yourself first, yet what is often missing is the 'How to!' and this book is full of very useful and practical techniques that are extremely easy to implement to help shift the stuck energy that can block our natural flow.

Through embracing her own authenticity and vulnerability, Andrea connects with the reader on a deep soul level as she candidly shares her own soul's journey to Acceptance & Self Love. This book is an *invitation to love the most important person in your life - YOU - so honour yourself and make the time to devour each page, you will be delighted that you did, I certainly was."*

— Jo Simpson, Founder of The Values Discovery Process, Executive Coach, Speaker and Author of *The Restless Executive*

"It could've been me! That's the feeling Andrea leaves me with all the time. And 'The Real Self Love Handbook' is no exception. I connect to Andrea and her writing because it is honest, it is open and it is courageous. And that's exactly the kind of mirror that helps me move forward in my own life. Tell me I'm not alone, tell me I'm not a freak and give me some tools to take it to the next level, baby!

If you are looking for fluff and hot air blown…somewhere, you've come to the wrong place. Andrea shares her candid, honest wisdom with us and for that, I truly am grateful."

— Helene Philipsen
Life Transformation Specialist
Creator of The Freedom from Emotional Eating Program
www.HelenePhilipsen.com

Also by Andrea Pennington

The Orgasm Prescription for Women: 21 Days to Heightened Pleasure, Deeper Intimacy and Orgasmic Bliss

How to Liberate and Love Your Authentic Self

The Top 10 Traits of Highly Resilient People

Daily Compassion Meditation: 21 Guided Meditations, Quotes and Images to Inspire Love, Joy and Peace

The Pennington Plan: 5 Simple Steps to Vibrant Health, Emotional Wellbeing and Spiritual Growth

Eat to Live: Protect Your Body + Brain + Beauty with Food

The Pennington Plan for Weight Success: 5 Steps to Permanent Weight Loss

Co-authored by Andrea Pennington

Magic and Miracles

Life After Trauma

Heart to Heart: The Path to Wellness

Resilience Through Yoga and Meditation

DEDICATION

This book is lovingly dedicated to my daughter, Siena.

*May you always know how precious and lovable you are.
May you continuously share your 'comic gold' and
unique character with zest.
You are truly the greatest gift to my life.*

*And to the longtime friend and supporter who saw the real me
and loved me unconditionally, even when I didn't love myself,
your continued presence in my life speaks volumes.*

CONTENTS

Acknowledgements

To my mother and father, whose instruction along the bumpy journey toward knowing and accepting myself has not always been obvious, but is sincerely appreciated.

I am truly grateful for the guidance, inspiration and loving support I receive from my clients, online community, family and friends on a daily basis. You all mean the world to me and make my 'job' feel like play!

I especially want to thank Janet Anthony, PhD who nudged, pleaded and urged me to get this book out to the world. I appreciate your lack of patience, for now this work can truly transform more lives. Thank you!

To Sister Jenna, who encouraged me to come out of my 'meditation cave' to be a force for good in the world, I appreciate your spiritual mentorship immensely.

Sincere thanks to Sólveig Þórarinsdóttir, Yvette Taylor and Deri Llewellyn-Davies, for entrusting me with your transformative programs, which I proudly share in this book and with everyone I meet. Your contributions to the world make an incredible difference and I'm honored to spread your messages globally.

I truly value the connection, inspiration and insights provided by my dear and wise colleagues Rúna Magnus, Gegga Birgis, Karena Virginia, Bitte Wiese, Gitte Winter Graugaard, Helene Philipsen, Halina Goldstein, Helen Rebello, Kitty Waters, Jo Simpson, Taz Thornton, Malin Hedlund, Willow McIntosh, Ofkje Teekens, Rob Goddard, Jill Stocker, Alexsa Covelli, Trevor Hahn and Nick Haines. You are all very precious to me!

My Invitation to You

I welcome you, dear reader, to join our global community of heart-centered, soul-inspired, conscious change makers at www.RealSelf.love

We are committed to supporting, inspiring and empowering one another on our collective mission to heal holistically, love wholeheartedly and live authentically.

Feeling social?
Join our private Facebook group at:
https://www.facebook.com/groups/RealSelfLoveMovement/

Foreword

Childhood can ignite magic. Childhood can ignite fear. As we grow into our adult lives, we are given the choice of which emotion to feed. It is easier for us to feed the magic if we grew up being accepted and celebrated for living into the brilliance of our destiny. However, if we were scolded for being too loud, dramatic or effervescent we may need a healing transformation of old belief systems and energy imprints in order to thrive into our adult years.

I was born in New York City in the early 1970's. Both my mother and father moved to America from England and Italy in the late 1960's. They met and fell madly in love. My father spoke only Italian until my British mother taught him to speak English. My father was bigger than life. He loved in a very deep and profound way. Somehow he was able to live his life in complete generosity even after growing up in Rome, Italy in a very poor family. He passed away in his sixties and everyday we miss him. I often wonder if his heart was too big for his physical landscape. Could his soul have been too vast for this world?

Mom is very proper. She is quite precious and delicate. Yet, she is also so very strong. She grew up during World War 2 where the fear of assault was present every day. However, she still emphasizes the importance of having good manners and being polite to the neighbors. Mom is a spiritual warrior and a benevolent volunteer all in one. With her British etiquette it is a bit uncomfortable for her to bring attention to the self by disrupting anything or anyone. So her warrior side is very quiet, but we know that warrior of love, light and empowerment lives inside mom. Sometimes the warrior hides in humility.

And she has me as her middle daughter.

I was born to create change. I had so much to say and such profound wisdom from the angels as a child. I used to sit with them and ask them why it was so hard being me. Why is everyone so different? Why do I feel and know things before they are revealed to the rest of the world? They used to tell me I was simply one of them. Only I was here and they were there.

When I was twelve I wanted to be with them so I prayed to get sick. It wasn't that my family did not love me, and it wasn't that I was abandoned or betrayed. It was the rejection and misunderstanding from being an empath in a world full of intellect. Having a destiny to shine so brightly that I would shine far and away scared me. Being connected to the mainstream was my only survival. So I faked enjoying cartoons. I pretended to read children's books. Meanwhile, my only focus was on God.

At twelve my prayer was answered and my appendix ruptured. That was my first near death experience. The only way to explain the love that the angels feel for all of us is to think of the love of a mother, multiply it by 100 and then take any of her fear away. Can you imagine the look in those eyes? Can you visualize that miraculous smile?

While spending most of my life playing small in order to fit into a society that often misunderstands empaths, and days varying between truly being me or not feeling worthy enough of being the enigmatic me, I have finally discovered the meaning of true self-love.

Self-love is recognizing that we are all gifts with different resonances, and together we create a beautiful harmony. True self-love is recognizing that we are who we are and that is that. I love me, too. After years of feeling shame for not conforming daily to the systems of society, I have finally made it home. Home is where my heart feels happy by beating tenderly in my body.

Andrea has created such a beautiful system in this amazing book. It is from Andrea's depth of heart, life experience's, medical training and profound soul full of spirit that her words flow.

May you find your path to true self-love. May you celebrate your worthiness and may you always remember how very loved you are.

From My Heart, with the tenderness of Love,
Karena Virginia
Spiritual Healer, Author, Empowerment Guru and Yogi

Introduction

Can you look in the mirror and say, "I love you, me"?

If you can look at yourself and fully accept that you are truly lovable right now, just as you are today — wrinkles, warts and all — then I'm sure you know how wonderful that freedom feels.

If you can't imagine saying those four words to yourself, stick with me. A few years ago, when I was facing severe depression, I would never have dreamed that I could say — or sing! — those words and mean them, but now I can. I can say them, even on a bad hair day, when I mess up at work, or say the wrong things. And yes, even when trolls criticize me or my content online.

I am here to tell you that you can have the same empowered feeling of freedom and true self-love. And it won't be difficult either. The Real Self Love Handbook will show you how.

In my first TEDx talk, in 2014, I outlined the 3 keys to manifesting your dreams into reality. After my talk, so many people told me how simple yet profound the message was. Then they asked what to do next. In this book you'll find my answer. I offer it to help you learn who you really are, love who you really are and live who you really are.

The steps that I took on my journey out of depression and anxiety were simple, but the path was a bit convoluted. In retrospect it seems deceptively obvious. I discovered an internal source of wisdom, peace and unconditional self-love that continues to nourish my heart and soul. I hid in the dark for so long that the joy I now feel to be free from depression is what inspires me to offer this process to you with the heartfelt desire that you, too, will find your inner bliss. Our inner bliss is something we all can create and access even if at times, we don't feel lovable.

In these pages I give you a guide, a 5-step framework for creating a stable foundation of real self-love. I've included principles from positive psychology, neuroscience, and ancient spiritual wisdom traditions that I've not only studied, but I've lived now for years. There is no religious dogma you have to adopt, but I often reference your "divine self." Getting to know the divine perfect self you truly are can set you free. And it can open the door to true healing of many forms of illness, disease, heartbreak and burnout. And it's a crucial part of becoming more resilient.

After years of therapy, trying antidepressants and anti-anxiety medication, practicing the Law of Attraction, reading self-help books and attending spiritual or personal development workshops I had given up on life. To my surprise, the depression completely vanished when I experienced first hand what philosophers, yogis, and spiritual masters have said for millennia is true — you are a perfect, whole, divine spiritual being with infinite potential. My aim is to provide you with a simple process for reconnecting to your Authentic Self and living with more power, passion, and purpose than ever before!

Now before you start thinking that I'm some positivity pushing, woo-woo New Age maniac, perhaps a bit of insight into the origins of the book and the awakening process I describe will be helpful to you. I'm into positivity, of course, but I wasn't always this way.

Every day I struggled to put on that happy smile before leaving the house to face the world. I had a deep sense of not being good enough, so I would strive to learn more facts, do more good, give more love, and achieve more goals.

How I Learned To Love and Be *The Real Me*

In August of 2005 I asked God to take my life.

After an impromptu vocal performance in a dreamy night club in St. Tropez, France, exhilarated but confused, I was ready for my life to be over. No, I wasn't drunk or drugged. I was so blissed out from temporarily living the life I *really* wanted, that I didn't want to go on living the miserable life I had before.

The irony is, from the outside, it appeared that I had an ideal life. Back in the United States I had a beautiful home, a stylish convertible car, a million-dollar business and plenty of famous friends. Only three years into my professional career I'd already published my first book, appeared on *Oprah* — *multiple times* — and I was seen on stages across America.

As "America's Empowerment Doctor" I was known for setting people free from disease, depression and dead-end careers. People came to see me from far and wide to help them heal and have a fabulous life, like mine. I regularly appeared in magazines and TV talk shows flashing a bright smile from ear to ear.

But that smile did not reflect true happiness. Not at all. On the inside I was miserable. Nobody could tell, of course. Because I hid it. When my career seemed to be at an all-time high and I had everything that one would consider worthwhile, I was utterly miserable. It was painful because I didn't like who I had become. My media image was that of a prudish know-it-all who wasn't following her own advice: "Honor your dreams, for they are the treasures of your soul."

Yeah, right! In truth I'm a performing artist with a medical degree — an actress who *played* a doctor on TV. Yet, I wasn't honoring *my* dream to sing, act, and perform. Instead I secretly lived with depression for over a decade.

Every day I struggled to put on that happy face before leaving the house to face the world. I had a deep sense of not being good enough, so I would strive to learn more facts, do more good, give more love, and achieve more goals. Despite being pursued by multiple suitors I couldn't seem to keep a relationship to save my life. My heart ached for love, the love and acceptance I didn't feel I deserved, but desperately wished for.

Many people are surprised to learn that I suffered from a lack of self-love and depression for decades. But it's true, I didn't love myself and I felt like a fraud.

My tactic to deal with the internal gloom was to achieve more success, attain more degrees and certifications, and accumulate more accolades for my work. I would give my time and money to family, friends, and charities — all of the things that our culture says will make us happy and honorable. However, when I achieved something great I'd see only the faults, the imperfections; all the places where I had fallen short of my ideal. After all the work and sacrifice I didn't even allow myself to enjoy the fruits of my labor. I didn't enjoy the mental or emotional boost of a job well done. Instead, fearing that my ego would get puffed up, I denied the brilliance of my accomplishments. Even while others cheered, applauded, and congratulated me, I never felt good enough. I didn't feel worthy of admiration.

Part of this tendency came from my childhood. When my parents divorced I was three years old. I missed my father terribly and we lived in different states so I only saw him a couple of times each year. My father, who grew up in a modest family, believed that getting an education and a "stable job" were the most important goals to achieve. He emphasized to me again and again that the only worthy goals for me were to study, get good grades, and go to university. When I did well in school it got me praise and positive attention from him.

Though I knew my father loved me in between the times when report cards came out, the pursuit of knowledge and a pattern of seeking achievement for praise was firmly engrained in my mental makeup. Needless to say, a great deal of the accomplishments in my life were initiated by my insatiable need for approval, first from my father, later from my medical colleagues, and finally from the media. The drive to succeed and to accumulate degrees, certifications, and honorable mentions was what motivated me. It was never-ending, unfulfilling and totally exhausting!

I hid behind a protective shell of doing, but I was dying inside.

To make matters worse, I never felt like I was good enough. I was plagued by the dreaded "Imposter Syndrome." I was constantly anxious and worried that someone would discover I didn't really know my stuff, that I was a fraud. I didn't dare show how pitiful I felt because I had made that mistake once before. I was met with looks of disbelief as those around me said I should be grateful for all that I had. I *was* grateful, but I didn't feel proud or fulfilled. My reputation for teaching and inspiring others left me isolated. I had no one to confess how I really felt. I hid behind a protective shell of doing, but I was dying inside.

Eventually, I realized that no matter how much I achieved, how much money I made, or how rich my personal lifestyle was it would always be society's ideal, not mine. So somewhere around age thirty, I began the several-year-long process of shedding my perfectionistic skin and stopped trying to live up to my father's ideal of accomplishment and success. I stopped doing things for the sake of looking good and relaxed my standards. I soon discovered that other things in life could bring me true joy and fulfillment. After years of therapy and soul-searching I learned that the depression I experienced wasn't solely linked to my insatiable childlike need for approval, nor was it purely biochemical. My sadness was also caused by my denial to fully express the desire of my soul to create and perform artistically.

To understand this better, let me take you back a few years in my timeline. Throughout my childhood I could be found on stage, on TV, or performing at my mother's house parties. This was the time when I felt most happy and fully alive. However, my father always told me that musicians and actors are a dime a dozen and that there were no guarantees that I could support myself as a performing artist. So as an adult I denied my soul its full creative expression. I held back the most passionate part of myself because I mistakenly believed that the arts were frivolous, and that being a healer would be more worthwhile. In my case, was I ever wrong!

Always curious and constantly researching my own journey of self-loathing, depression, and anxiety, led me to ask a lot of questions about life and love. While searching for relief from my own mental anguish I hit rock bottom and I cried out to the Divine for help. It was during a serious emotional low point in 2005, my "dark night of the *ego*." My life felt like a lie, except for one glorious night in the South of France. I was on a retreat-style vacation where, in true artist fashion, I courageously sang my heart out to a club of partygoers who didn't know my name or boring US TV image. It was pure bliss! And it was a far cry from the boring routine I lived back in the US, the very dim life I was set to return to in a matter of days.

Following the ecstasy of entertaining as my most bold self I returned to my hotel room in Cannes. All alone, the familiar dark mood returned when I realized that in just two days I'd have to return to my life in America.

It was then that I cried out to God to take it all — my body, talents, and business. I sobbed, "I don't know what I'm doing with my life! YOU take it!"

I was wracked with an intense longing for meaning, a glimmer of joy, and some kind of relief. I wasn't suicidal, I would not have harmed myself. But I did want out of my personal pain. In total despair, I sobbed and flung myself onto the bed; my body trembled intensely. What happened next was a mystical, out of body, near-death-like experience where I thought God was answering my prayer to end my life.

My Near-Death-Like Experience and the End Of the Old Me

I felt as though I'd melted into the bed and an immense feeling of inner peace overtook me. Shaking, crying, and desperately praying for relief, I suddenly saw an all-consuming, intense white light. Confused, thinking the sun in Cannes couldn't possibly get any brighter, I squinted, trying to find the source of the light. To my surprise it was coming from *inside* me. I felt myself being drawn into the light as my body seemed to disappear.

I no longer felt like *me*. I was aware of the concept of *Andrea Pennington*, but I felt *more* than she. I felt complete Oneness and absolute, pure love. I felt love for myself and all of existence. It was the most beautiful feeling of calm and peace. My struggle to feel better seemed to finally come to a serene end. The awareness I gained caused an instantaneous shift in my entire existence.

Though unseen, I sensed the presence of a non-physical loving being next to me. From a detached perspective I saw an overview of my entire life, in an instant. As it flashed before me, I understood how each of my choices led me to my depressive state. No explanations were needed. I simply knew the source of my overwhelming sense of misery. It was so comforting to be free from the pain of life.

Several important lessons were shown to me that totally set me free, which I now share with you (and anyone who will listen) to give you the keys to your own freedom. There are several insights, which came with such clarity that they need to stand alone to be appreciated, so I will sprinkle them throughout the pages of this book. For now, these are a few realizations, or Truths, that bear knowing up front.

1. From that expanded state of awareness, I realized that in life on Earth, there is a Spirit, Source energy, Love or pure consciousness, which inhabits all things. And I saw and experienced how I am one with, united with that spirit or consciousness. In fact, no matter how separate we may feel at times, I saw that *we are all one* with that consciousness.

2. Though I am one with all consciousness I have my own spirit or higher self that is aware of every minute of my present and each of my past lifetimes. It also knows the cause of my present, past, and future troubles, and triumphs.

3. In addition to my spirit, I also have my own life essence — a soul. The human soul is an accumulation of past experiences, karma and genetic information passed down through time. Each soul has particular tendencies and preferences, which I call the "spiritual DNA."

4. My spirit is meant to be in control of my life as a human being. And as a co-creator of my life on earth, I am free to become what *I* choose — whether consciously or unconsciously. The earthly expression of my spiritual essence is totally of *my* choosing and that there is no "wrongness" in my choice. There is no God judging me, but my actions bear fruit and

consequences. When I am ready, my spirit can even help me transcend or go beyond my past programming — both the programming I received during this lifetime, and even past lifetimes of soul programming and agreements.

5. As my true self is spirit and as an offshoot of pure consciousness, I am totally lovable, perfect, and complete. No matter the drama, trauma or karma my soul has accumulated or endured — at our core we are all truly lovable.

During that out of body experience I realized that my whole life had been leading me to one major realization, something that our spirit knows all along: in order to enjoy a life of total wellness and happiness on earth we must become and express who we *really* are — not who our parents, society, or religion force us to be. None of our past programming, life experience, or trauma dictates, or limits who we are or who we can become.

The understanding of these principles was instantaneous and certain. I felt with complete assuredness that to live a life of freedom and joy, we can align our actions with our spirit, rather than the ego or programs of the soul. To do so we must *learn* who we *really* are, *love* who we are and *live* who we are. We are creators of life, including our own.

In that state of bliss, another stream of messages flowed to me and I was filled with a quiet joyful sense of well-being. Here are a few more of the messages, which eased my emotional pain instantly. They are critical to you understanding the material in this book:

1. It's normal to want to be seen for who we are, that's why we came to play in this game of life on earth. We all want to be embraced and cherished for who we *really* are, that's our birthright. We all want to express ourselves wholeheartedly and to share ourselves meaningfully with others, that is our soul's greatest desire.

2. True happiness comes from within and it comes naturally when we integrate our whole being — mind, body, spirit, and soul.

3. We are all born with a deep desire to have an impact in the world, and to feel fulfilled knowing that we make a difference because deep down, our spirit reminds us that we DO matter.

4. You are a divine spiritual being with a perfect soul.

5. In this life you are meant to express your true feelings and desires.

6. You are meant to embody your soul's consciousness in your own chosen way in the precious human body you were given.

7. You are entitled to enjoy the unique talents, gifts, and body you've been given. You are meant to thrive and to live life fully.

8. You are inherently perfect just as you are, just like the day you were born. Despite the errors you may have made, and the self-judgments and erroneous beliefs that hide your soul's light, the perfect, whole, lovable Light that you truly are still shines. No matter your looks, no matter your behavior, you are magnificent, just as you are!

I hope these messages give you comfort, as they did for me. I realized that I'm not wrong, bad, or selfish for wanting to feel like I matter and for wanting to be seen for who I really am.

As I allowed the peace of Oneness to bypass and replace all my previous thinking and biases, a vision of myself appeared in my awareness. I saw myself living joyfully on the French Riviera. In this vision of a new life I was with a child, I was singing professionally and I could heal people with my hands. Though stunned by the bizarreness of this life vision, I was inspired. In fact, I felt a total acceptance to return to my life, but with renewed enthusiasm to live according to my deepest desires. I said, "Yes" to Life and a few days later I returned to America a changed woman. There was no returning to the inauthentic version of me!

No matter how separate we may feel at times, we are all one with pure consciousness.

"What *Really* Happened To Me?"

Curious and hungry to understand what I'd experienced, I gradually withdrew from the media limelight to allow my new reality to fully integrate and get to know the real me. Little by little I let go of my high octane career and embarked on a serious journey of self-discovery, which included deep meditation, qigong, and a rigorous practice of self-inquiry. This enabled me to get to the bottom of the source of my emotional pain.

I was inspired to plunge into research of near-death experiences. I studied the neuropsychology of consciousness and read classic books by early mystics. I met with shamans, a Mexican curandera (healer) and meditation masters. I wanted to understand how I could be so thoroughly transformed, happy, and peaceful so instantly and so completely.

It filled me with joy to learn that many cultures have taught these same concepts. So many native and indigenous traditions recognize these concepts as obvious and worth following. As a result, they don't have the types of existential angst that I had.

My new quest for self-discovery led me to question everything I'd thought was true and everything upon which I had built my life. As I explored my family of origin it was easy to see how I'd been programmed into conformity and taught to distrust my own heart. My father's insistence that a career in the arts wasn't a reliable way to support myself and his advice to pursue higher education drove my artistic passion into hiding. In fact, every time I wanted to sing or create for art's sake, I felt self-loathing and shame well up within me. I was driven to achieve academically and professionally to the detriment of my dreams. I learned to trust the opinions of others rather than the nudging of my own heart and spirit. I became who I thought I needed to be for acceptance. But what I became was only a fragment of the real me.

What I found out, was that before my experience with Oneness, I didn't believe I was worthy of love if I wasn't "perfect" in every way. I also uncovered hidden shame I felt for mistakes from the past which I still carried in my heart that impacted my romantic relationships and business pursuits. As much as I wanted success or to connect deeply with the men I was dating, I would unconsciously sabotage things.

Through the practice of inquiry, meditation, and self-compassion I finally found peace and unconditional self-acceptance. Maybe not all of the time, but much more often than before. Recognizing the hidden influences that have shaped my behavior has allowed me to be more understanding and kind to myself. I've learned to love myself just as I am, especially because of *how* I am.

Now I fully accept and apply my tendency toward perfectionism, my flair for dramatic presentations, and my nerdy drive to compile and teach medical and psychological research for the empowerment of anyone who will listen! I occasionally have periods of emotional upset, but nothing that has driven me to hide in shame. At least not for long, anyway.

Of course, my story is not unique. I'd bet at one point in your life you've felt the same, haven't you?

We've all been conditioned to live inside of a predefined set of rules and expectations and forced to fit inside a box. The programming of our self-image begins in childhood, so let's explore that process now. Your understanding of how natural it is to take on the programs thrust upon us will empower you to change the programs that do not serve you.

Being welcomed into the 'in' crowd often means giving up your personal ideals in favor of the majority.

Birth of the M'Ego

From the time we are born, the immature ego personality is formed and struggles to manage our behaviors—balancing desire for self-expression, while seeking approval and acceptance from others. Through the socialization process we take on the beliefs of others that can cause our own self-rejection and self-loathing. We mold and fold ourselves into the ideal form or function we believe will help us be accepted. We create, unconsciously of course, a version of "me" we present to the world. (I like to call it the m'ego because as children we associate this facade as "me" even though it's a construct built upon experience. I also prefer m'ego to avoid confusion with the commonly used concept of ego as just a big, confident attitude.)

I've always known that I had some psychic abilities, even as a child. I would never tell people that because I thought it was weird that I knew things before others did, or that I could sense new trends and occurrences without visible, physical facts. Instead of being labeled a 'freak,' I tried harder to fit in. Conformity has a high price though. Being welcomed into the 'in' crowd often means giving up your personal ideals in favor of the majority. The m'ego quickly learns what one should and should not do for the continued acceptance and favor of others. Sometimes we forfeit our individuality and creative self-expression. Which is such a shame, since we each came to this lovely blue planet to share our unique presence with the world.

In my case, I had a gut instinct that my purpose in life was somewhere outside the box I was living in, but I was afraid to break away from the 'safe' life I had constructed. I resisted my innate tendencies for artistic self-expression and ended up masquerading as a half-baked version of myself. The mask of m'ego became hard to take off. Conforming to the various groups I was surrounded by led me to a profound depression.

Progressive Self-Rejection

The artist in me, when allowed to play and perform, helps me to enter the flow state where I feel blissfully whole and perfect, just as I am. Yet for years my programming plummeted me into self-rejection, shame, and sadness when strong urges of creative self-expression welled up within me. Self-denial led to an anxious tension that permeated everything I did. And then this nervous energy infected my relationships, work and everyday life. Constantly checking to see if I was fitting in, I drove the seemingly unacceptable parts of my personality into the shadows. The m'ego almost suffocated my true identity. (Fortunately, the Authentic Self is incredibly resilient and can't be snuffed out permanently!)

The early years of my adult life were spent struggling against expressing my true nature and deep interests and fitting into my everyday world. To deal with the painful longing for wholehearted acceptance I felt, I compensated with more achievement and education. I blocked so many of my soul's attempts for play, as if I were unworthy of simple joy. In retrospect, looking over my medical career I see how clearly some of my patients' lack of self-love led them to sabotage their addiction recovery or weight loss efforts.

Can you relate to this in any way?

I have since learned that not living in and expressing our true potential can lead to feeling hopeless and miserable. Though we may be highly functional, we are not fulfilled. And despite our success, we're not satisfied. Limited by low self-confidence, many of us use our life circumstances to justify not taking action when it's really our own fear of rejection, judgment, failure, or fear of success. Instead of reaching for our dreams we compromise and find it easier to surrender to predefined roles and expectations.

But there comes a time when we must say, "enough is enough!" The desire to break free and live a new way becomes stronger than our fear. The spirit within, stirs us into action. I hope that it is your time to rise right now.

Along my journey, after the out-of-body experience, I learned that our natural strengths can be used to revive the true self. We can rewrite our self-description and recreate our self-image as *we* desire to be. We then have the power to rebuild our lives as the living temple of our Authentic Self.

Read on to find out how I did it, so that you can, too.

My Renaissance

After cutting the ties with my former way of life I began an intensive meditation, yoga, and qigong practice. I did eventually move to France, my young daughter by my side. Through deep introspection and living from my strengths, passions, dreams, and desires I now feel confident in who I am. Anchored in my Truth I have consciously constructed my life and career *on my terms*. I now truly love myself and enjoy greater well-being than I thought possible! I am living my Diamond Life.

I don't think you need to move to a foreign country, perform onstage, or have an out-of-body near-death-like experience to learn — or remember — that you are totally lovable as you are. My path was quite a convoluted adventure to total wellness and personal fulfillment. I've since discovered that by following a few simple steps, you can reconnect with your Authentic Self, which is like returning to your true home. This book outlines those steps for you. And in our free online training program, you can get my video guidance as you implement the 5-Step Cornerstone Process. Join for free at www.RealSelf.love

I hope that sharing my story shows you that when you listen to and trust the guidance and wisdom from your spirit, your true nature can be allowed to flourish. It's then that innovation and creativity will outweigh the tendency toward conformity and competition. Peace, joy, and inner harmony can naturally outweigh frustration, depression, and addiction. And from that place of inner harmony and unconditional self-acceptance, you may also find that your physical wellbeing and vitality is restored as well.

My passion is to empower you to live authentically with purpose and passion by discovering and embracing your unique, Authentic Self, and living in alignment with spirit to become who you *really* are. I believe this is the way to consciously create a life filled with meaning, power, and fulfillment. This is how you'll have an extraordinary impact in the world.

And the world desperately needs *your* authentic, original life expression. We are part of an interconnected living organism and what you do individually matters to us collectively. Your personality, character, values, and talents are all unique and they are essential to the health and well-being of you individually and to the whole of humanity. You are a gift to the world!

I welcome you to join a community of conscious people who are also dedicated to bringing more love, joy and Light to the planet. Visit www.RealSelf.Love for more information.

Much love,
Dr. Andrea
Cannes, France

The Cornerstone Process

5 Steps to Real Self-Love

When I gave my first TEDx talk in 2014, I outlined 3 keys to transforming your dreams into reality. To live a life you love, you must 1) know your true self, 2) love and nurture yourself (body, mind, and spirit), and 3) begin living with purpose as your Authentic Self. To live in this way sets you up for a life of discovery, adventure, growth, and meaning.

Over the last decade I have taught 5 steps or core principles, which provide a framework for gentle self-love and life mastery, it's called The Cornerstone Process. With continued use and reflection you'll find that The Cornerstone Process can become a natural part of your lifestyle on your path to awakened living.

The 5 steps are:

1. **Awareness**

2. **Acceptance**

3. **Accountability**

4. **Inspired Action**

5. **Appreciation**

Working with this process has proven effective for me personally, as well as for my colleagues, and my clients. Following this framework can stimulate and inspire your awakening, set you free from addictive patterns, and help you align with your deepest desires, ideals, and motivations to live a full, abundant, healthy life. This approach to self-awareness also leads to immense inner peace and acceptance.

I will walk you through each step of the process and offer practical tips on how to apply it in your life starting today. Applying the process over time will enable you to fill your heart with love and deep appreciation for life.

Love doesn't have to be earned, you don't have to wait for someone to give it to you, and you can never be found undeserving of it.

Love is never in short supply. It is abundant, inexhaustible, easily accessed and FREE!

Imagine Being Happily in Love with YOU

If you've ever been in romantic love then you know how exciting, fulfilling, and fun it is to do things with and for your beloved. Outside of romantic love, parents and grandparents also describe the immense joy of showering love, gifts, and all types of treats on their precious little ones. Love can inspire you to get up early, stay up late, sit through boring movies, read the same bedtime story for the fiftieth time, and much more just to please or pamper your beloved.

Love elevates us to higher states of being that bring out the best, most generous parts of us. Nothing can stop you from seeing the best in your loved one and forgiveness comes easily with unconditional love. When you're infused with the energy of love you're motivated to be your best and do your best, not just for the recipient of your love but often for everyone and everything around you. It's as if your love bubbles up out of your heart and touches everyone with joy, acceptance, and peace. This unconditional love also touches them on a deeply emotional level, and can elevate their bad moods or gloomy thoughts. Love is truly magical in that way.

The power of love has been shown to reverse illness, speed recovery and healing, inspire creativity, attract loving partners, magnetize good fortune and prosperity, and stimulate creativity, peace and overall well-being. *Love is the very essence of life.* It sustains all living things and permeates all the cells in your body. Best of all, despite what your past may have shown you, love doesn't have to be earned, you don't have to wait for someone to give it to you, and you can *never* be found undeserving of it. Love is never in short supply. It is abundant, inexhaustible, easily accessed and FREE!

The life enhancing energy and magic of love surrounds us and is available at every moment — even when we are alone or not 'in love' with someone. In addition to self-discovery the principles in this book will teach you how to access and channel the magnificent power of unconditional love to energize and heal yourself, give your life more meaning, purpose, and fulfillment, and ultimately, transform the world around you. And right now, that's just what we need the most!

Love Can Help Us Heal The World

The world today has come to a point of such devastation, instability, and chaos that many of us have realized that solutions to the global problems affecting billions must lie within some higher intelligence and wisdom. That very intelligence and wisdom flows through your heart — it's love.

When we are motivated by love we are unstoppable. There's nothing that cannot be solved, healed, or transformed. My goal is to help you increase your capacity for love — starting with yourself — and your ability to use love's power to heal the world, starting with the people, places, and circumstances closest to you.

When you are turned on by love, you will turn others on, too. When you love and accept yourself, you become supercharged and attuned to your destiny, allowing you to move through life gracefully to fulfill it.

It's Time to Build Your Life On A Foundation of Real Self-Love

Master bricklayers know that when laying the foundation for a new building the cornerstone must be carefully laid to provide stability. Each of us also needs a cornerstone of true self-love to form a strong and secure foundation for our life journey.

With nearly twenty years of practicing holistic integrative medicine I've discovered that it doesn't matter how many acupuncture needles, pills, surgeries, procedures, or hours of psychotherapy a client undergoes, if they lack a fundamental base of real self-love their health may improve temporarily, but ultimately, they often return to some level of *dis*-ease. Self-sabotage or just giving up comes naturally to those who do not value themselves and to those who don't feel lovable.

Love is like the nourishing rain that keeps us growing — even when weeds, stones and pests disturb our otherwise peaceful garden.

Just as when we truly love another, when we love ourself we want the best outcome, the best health, the best food, the best state of being for ourself. When we love another unconditionally our goal is for our beloved to be happy and free. When you are brimming and overflowing with unconditional love for yourself you'll freely live an incredibly powerful and purposeful life in optimal health and well-being. Nothing will stop you from pursuing your highest goals and ideals, realizing your greatest potential, and living with authentic happiness and integrity. And this will empower you to be a loving, generous contribution to others and all inhabitants on earth.

Love truly conquers all. Not through destructive force, however. Love brings light, harmony, and grace. Negativity, chaos, and sickness are diminished in the presence of love. All things are returned to their original state of perfection and order when love is present. Once that loving light infuses your being and you are returned to the 'original source code program' for your life, you'll see all areas of your life align themselves in miraculous ways to support the highest expression of you.

Laying down your own cornerstone of self-love is not a frivolous, selfish, or narcissistic thing. By prioritizing your own self-acceptance you'll be better equipped to generously love, support, and give to others. Loving yourself is both natural and healthy and contributes to a ripple effect in the universe, and in the world.

Real Self-love Is Your Birthright

When you were born, you deserved the best life possible. You had the right to express yourself fully and the right to grow and evolve into a complete and functional human. Before the outer world began programming your subconscious mind through the socialization process, there was an original program that held the information or blueprint of your perfect potential for vitality, success, and happiness. Before you took on the judgments, beliefs, biases, and self-doubts of the world, you existed in a state of full self-worth and true self-love.

You are entitled to enjoy that previous state of love for yourself NOW and into the future!

The real you is still totally in love with your true spiritual essence — the real You. You just have to recognize it.

What gets in the way of our natural, healthy self-acceptance? Social, political, and religious conditioning, media brainwashing, family programming, and life experiences. But as much as our original self may have been molded, shaped, hidden, or crammed into a box, we can uncover it, reawaken our true nature, and live in alignment with our values on our own terms. It's never too late!

Master bricklayers know that when laying the foundation for a new building the cornerstone must be carefully laid to provide stability.

The Structure of This Book

My intention is to provide you with the framework, guidance, and inspiration to *learn* who you are, *love* who you are, and *live* who you are. The 5-step Cornerstone Process will allow you to tap into your personal truths, the truths that point the way to embracing your natural gifts and sharing them with the world in a meaningful way.

Part 1 will help you *learn who you* really *are.* A variety of exercises and self-inquiry will help you remember and recognize your original self. You'll discover your innate lovability as we uncover the false beliefs that made you *think* you weren't lovable in the first place. Only once we've cleared away the debris of past programming, can we begin to consciously lay your Cornerstone of enduring self-love.

In Part 2 we move into the healing and energy-clearing phase so that you unconditionally *accept* and truly *love who you are.* You will learn to *attune* to the field of unconditional love and limitless potential to consciously create a life worth living.

Finally, in Part 3 we explore how to *live who you really are* by embracing your strengths and talents and bringing them to every area of your life work, play, relationships, and personal development.

I will include elements from my life journey as well as my nerdy discoveries from the world of neuroscience, positive psychology, and the various wisdom traditions I have explored. There is no religion promoted in this book, so no matter your beliefs on that front, nothing presented here will interfere with your spiritual tradition. In fact, both atheist and religious scholars alike have told me that the insights presented here are aligned with the deepest truths held for millennia.

PART I

AWAKEN: LEARN WHO YOU *REALLY* ARE

The Cornerstone Process
Step 1 — Awareness

Who am I, *really*?

To allow the Cornerstone of self-love to take its rightful place in your psyche and life we will begin with the first step: **Awareness**. To love yourself you must know yourself, so your first priority is to become aware of who you *really* are — or who you are *intended* to be. You'll become aware of your true nature through a process of self-inquiry and self-discovery aided by several questionnaires, exercises, and activities that will shine light on the Real You — strengths, weaknesses, limitations, and ideals.

The science of positive psychology has informed a great deal of my work. This scientific approach to happiness shifts the focus from what's wrong in humans to the positive qualities in us that help us flourish and thrive. I believe the tenets of positive psychology can lead us out of the painful existence of conformity and mediocrity into a bright future of healthy interdependence, success and creativity.

Many of your present strengths, interests, and talents are evidence of an original spiritual imprint that precedes your social programming. That spiritual imprint is the source code for the real you. Though some of your innate qualities may have been hidden, squashed, or invalidated, they can be reignited, reinvigorated, and reclaimed. To know that you are part of the perfect field of consciousness with a particular set of contributions to make, roles to perform, and experiences to live, is part of your liberation to be who you want to be — not who you were forced, coerced, or molded to be.

In Step 1, in addition to exploring your strengths we'll also explore your core beliefs to enhance your self-awareness. We will expose areas of doubt that may be keeping you locked into patterns, habits, or life choices that are dis-empowering. Like debugging a computer of malware or viruses, all of the limiting beliefs and mental concepts hidden in your mind that are not in line with a life of joy, vitality and harmony will be removed by working through The Cornerstone Process.

We'll also examine your family history, temperament, and personality to become aware of the physical and mental aspects of you and how the sense of a separate, distinctive 'I' came to be. As you discover your signature strengths and values in action, which point to the inherent good in you, the essential building blocks of your architectural plan for awakened living will be revealed.

In Step 1 you'll also discover the value of becoming mindful of and naming what you feel, see, and hear in our body-mind — rather than hiding from, denying, stuffing, or medicating our painful emotions with drugs, food, sex, shopping or mindless activities.

As you become aware of the ways in which your true nature has been with you all along, even if it was suppressed or quietly waiting in the background of your everyday life, you'll find it easier to move on to the second step: **Acceptance.**

1

Discover the Real You

To love who you really are you must know who you really are.
The authentic you is totally lovable!

Have you ever wondered who you would be if you'd always been allowed to do what *really* interested you since the time you were born? I don't mean if you were spoiled by getting every toy or doll. I mean, how different would your self-image be if you could've followed every dream or desire straight through without second-guessing yourself or being suppressed by others? Can you even imagine what life would've been like if you'd been free to explore without judging your creative urges against what your peers, family members, church or society told you were acceptable? What career path would you have *naturally* chosen? What types of friends and intimate relationships would you have enjoyed if you were faithful to the desires of the *real* you?

To begin the wonderful discovery of who you really are you must first uncover the hidden internal influences that have been present since your birth. No matter how brainwashed you've been by the media, a coercive parent, spouse, or by religion, you can uncover clues to the real you, the you that you already are.

Little traces of the real you are present today in your
personality, your character and your deepest dreams.

Simple steps toward awakening the Authentic Self

Many of us think that who we are is a reflection of what we see in the mirror, the entries on our resume, what we try to portray to others, or what we aspire to be based on our parents' hopes and dreams. Based on this assumed self we see staring back at us, it's easy to see why we struggle to love ourselves. This accumulation of experiences, stories, hurts, failures, shortcomings and comparisons contradicts all notions of lovability!

But have you ever sensed that there is more to you than what you see reflected in the mirror?

In my first TEDx talk, 'Become Who You Are', I told the audience about how the Greek philosopher, Aristotle, said that we all have a telos. The telos is the endpoint to which we are aiming. And in Aristotle's view, **the end goal of life is to discover the self**. This is the self-awareness that can set you free.

The Ancient Greek lyric poet, Pindar, made things even more clear. He is famed for saying "Become such as you are, having learnt what that is." Pindar implied that **we can only become who we are if we've done the work to discover ourself**. This implies the possibility of deep self-knowledge, a recognition that there is more to you than what you see in the mirror.

It's time to learn who you really are, so you can become who you really are. There is more to you than your list of accomplishments — or failures. There is even a core part of you that is connected to every other being on earth. There is a part of you that is more pure, perfect, strong, and whole than the little human mind can conceive. There is actually a part of you that is superhuman, Divine and complete. This is the real YOU, your Authentic Self.

In order to live a life that is filled with happiness and fulfillment we must come to know the presence of and recognize the value of our Authentic Self. The first step is to recognize that you are **beyond** what you see in the mirror. There is an essence, spirit, or Authentic Self that lies hidden beneath the surface of the social mask you wear.

Seeing beyond the personality

For some, the biggest challenge is to recognize the hidden self behind the veil of the m'ego. You must remind yourself that the ego is an illusion created through the complex socialization process. In other words, it is not a solid, fixed identity. By mistaking your true self with the created social entity known as the m'ego, you may get stuck in undesirable life situations and emotional states. The good news is that once you recognize that your m'ego is not YOU, you are one step closer to freedom, this is part of your awakening to Truth.

Make a list of the times in life you've felt a deep knowing, intuition or strong feeling that you were more than just a skin encapsulated personality. Was it while looking at a newborn baby, being a witness to the beauty in nature, in sports, or in love? Write down any observations you've had in life that have led you to question whether your physical presence is all that there is.

_____

_____

_____

_____

_____

_____

_____

_____

_____

_____

_____

_____

_____

_____

If you've already had this type of personal awakening you were probably left wondering, *now what?* I believe that after becoming aware of who you really are — which is formless, timeless, eternal and NOT the m'ego — you can embark on your journey to healing and ultimately to true self-love.

After the epiphany, what comes next?

After your personal "aha moment" how do you move from painfully suffering through tragedy to joyfully living your destiny? How do you transform your perception of painful life lessons into the joy of life's blessings?

My own experience and research have shown me that you can integrate a mental or spiritual awakening into your daily life that will lead to the continued unfolding of love, joy, and peace. (By daily life I mean work, taking care of the kids, maintaining a household, and handling everyday, ordinary demands.)

The core principles of the holistic self-discovery process outlined in this book will serve as a helpful framework for what may be a lifelong journey of transformation. You can consider The Cornerstone Process to be a guide, much like what Abraham Maslow suggested in his famous hierarchy of needs which lead to self-actualization.

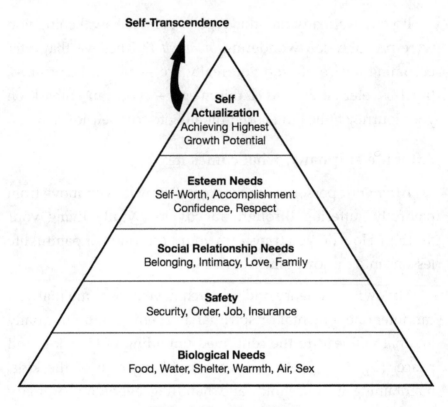

Maslow's Hierarchy of Needs

Self-Actualization

In 1943, American psychologist, Abraham Maslow wrote a paper published in *Psychological Review* where he outlined a hierarchy of human needs. He explained that our drive to fulfill our needs starts with the basic Biologic and Physiological Needs such as the need for shelter, food, air, water, warmth and sleep.

Once the basic physical needs are met one can then move up to the Safety Needs, which include security, stability, and order. We pursue things that bring a sense of stability or insurance through our job or connections.

As the needs for safety and security are met we tend to naturally feel a pull toward finding love and belonging, the so-called Social Relationship Needs. The desire to fulfill our longing for family, intimacy and love are here.

Next comes the Esteem Needs, which includes the need to be recognized as competent by oneself and by others. Self-worth, accomplishment and respect is involved here and expands to a need for cognitive or intellectual stimulation and exploration. Expanding more, we move into esthetic needs such as a desire for harmony, order, and beauty.

If all of those lower needs are met, or we feel confident in our pursuit of them, we may finally arrive at the need for Self-Actualization where we are engaged in or pursue activities which allow us to fully achieve and express our full potential. With regard to self-actualization, Maslow expressed it beautifully in this way, "the need to become everything that one is capable of becoming" eventually becomes all consuming. The writer must write; the painter must paint; the dancer must dance, if they are to be at peace with themselves.

The final stage is variable and highly dependent on each individual. Maslow recognized that we each have a sovereign self that is entitled to its own opinions, preferences, and values. This is why we do not naturally feel compelled by the same pursuits as everyone else, including our parents. (In this book I refer to our actualized sovereign self as the Authentic Self.)

Maslow also noticed that without being consumed with meeting our basic needs, the self-actualized person, at the height of their personality development, will often experience moments of profound love, insight, happiness, or rapture in which we feel more alive, whole, and connected to the world. During what he called peak experiences we become tuned into the goodness, harmony, truth, justice, and beauty that exists in life. And we sense that life is about more than our limited sense of self.

I believe, as did Maslow, that when we are fortunate enough to know our sovereign self, when we express ourselves openly and authentically, while working and playing from our full potential, we experience more of these peak experiences and more flow. We discover that the bliss, joy, and "in the zone" feeling of flow is motivation enough to keep exploring and growing. Without an overt agenda, we are inspired to use our skills and talents with passion, and in many cases, without concern for a specific outcome. To live a life fully engaged, present and inspired is what a self-actualized life could look like.

It doesn't end there, however.

Self-Transcendence

Beyond self-awareness and self-actualization, you can also step onto a path toward self-transcendence. To transcend means to go beyond. Self-transcendence means you are motivated to move beyond the obsessive drive of need fulfillment of the lower self, or m'ego. To go beyond the mundane pursuits of food, shelter, acceptance, fame, and material success to connect with a greater purpose beyond yourself is to transcend the lower self. It is often those peak experiences of flow, seen when we live and express our Authentic Self that we recognize our potential to transcend, to go beyond the m'ego and to merge into a collective earth family.

In fact, it's now believed that we all have an innate drive to experience a sense of connectedness with our planet, with all people, and all life. We can awaken to this internal drive for creating a life of deep meaning, sharing, and loving. When we do this is what will ultimately make the world a better place for *everyone* and will give each of us a sense that life is finally worth living. This drive, however, is often only felt when our lower needs are met. And though it is an inborn aspect of humanity, it can be ignored or overridden.

Tumbling down the pyramid

Some people struggle to attain the higher levels of personal mastery shown in Maslow's hierarchy depicted in the pyramid. Sadly some people don't reach a point of self-actualization nor do all people feel the drive for self-transcendence. Instead, rather than progressing onward and upward, some of us, as if sleep-walking, get stuck in a rut of self-defeating behaviors, competitiveness, greed, or over-indulgence. Often it's due to a traumatic experience or extreme need deprivation that will cause some people to forgo pursuing the higher needs. Instead they embark on a self-limiting circuit of the pursuit of food, sex, or acquiring more symbols of wealth. Rather than move up toward fulfillment of personal needs of self-actualization and self-transcendence, they tumble down the pyramid to continually pursue again more basic needs.

It's as if they are stuck in a pursuit of lower needs because their mind doesn't recognize that they've safely attained them before, or because they simply do not have the personal strength, belief or determination to go higher. The m'ego, with its focus on survival turned on hyperdrive, creates a disconnection from a deeper sense of self. This may cause some people to substitute physical needs over our deeper spiritual need to evolve and grow.

Have you known anyone who has such a deep sense of scarcity or lack that they stockpile or hoard resources? It is as if the brain never gets the message of 'enough' and they feel the need to stockpile anything from food to extra socks. Their sense of insecurity for the lower needs being met prevents them from tuning into the drive to progress.

Or have you known someone who grew up with an emotionally distant parent who has such a desperate need for connection and intimacy that they sought to 'plug in' to anyone they could? When our lower needs are not met, due to life circumstances, inadequate resources in childhood or breakdowns along life's journey, it can override our internal drive to accomplish and achieve self-mastery. This is a devastating turn of events — if we do not become conscious of what's happened to us.

Sometimes waking up to realize that our obsessions, behaviors, and tendencies are self-destructive habits, provides the impetus to look for more out of life.

The struggles we experience in life can be painful, troublesome moments of crisis or they can be opportunities for breakthroughs in our personal evolution. When we recognize that we are not progressing in a forward moving fashion toward actualization of the Authentic Self, this can be a perfect time to investigate our life patterns and internal beliefs. Some experiences may have cut us off from or prevented us from listening to our higher self's urge for progress, but we can correct those false assumptions and heal old wounds. We can get back on track with our soul's evolutionary program by remembering and reconnecting to who we really are.

Before we move toward reclaiming the parts of you that may have been suppressed or hidden, the first question we must answer is: How did we get here? While I've already suggested common ways we may get off track, let's explore the early childhood development principles. Don't worry, this will be useful for you now and in the future.

Psychologists tell us that the development of our self-image, our ego, begins during the first three years of life. So, let's revisit the beginning, your birth.

From the critical moment a child begins to sense that she is separate from her mother the process of programming begins.

The Anatomy of Your Self-image

In the womb, a baby begins in a pure, holistic environment of unconditional love where all of her needs are met instantly. She floats in a warm bath of comfort, safety, and protection. With few exceptions, like being a twin or triplet, she has plenty of room to stretch and grow as she needs. Her mother's heartbeat and voice provide soothing, reassuring sounds that tell her she is connected to a steady source of life. She and Mommy are one.

At birth the human infant has no sense of a separate self. She is pure Being. She has no concept of herself as a separate entity, and has no individual self-consciousness. The sense of a separate self develops gradually, from the interaction with her environment, particularly with her mother or other primary caretakers.

At birth our perfect little human moves to an external environment that is often quite harsh in comparison to her mother's womb. Life outside of Mommy can be an uncomfortable place where, for example, the temperature is not always consistent, and the warm amniotic bath has been replaced by scratchy, dry textures. Worse yet, it's noisy and bumpy out there. She now also feels physical sensations of lack (hunger) and notices the absence of Mother's heartbeat and warmth from time to time. To satisfy new pangs of hunger or to relieve her discomfort sometimes she instinctively cries out for nourishment, connection, and soothing.

Our little human baby quickly learns that she has 'needs' and must express herself to get what she requires. When those needs are met by what she soon realizes is a hand, bottle, breast, or lap, *external* to herself, she begins to perceive 'other' and 'me.' Her sense of self develops through the creation of internalized sensations of herself and the external perceptions of the other. Slowly, through experiences of apparent isolation, pleasure, and pain, memory traces are retained, forming the first self-impressions. The child begins to recognize that 'me' is different from 'you.' This is how the ego-identity and sense of self develop and become stable. Over time, the self-image, or ego, will regulate behaviors and manage emotions in attempt to satisfy the needs and desires of the individual.

The ego is a part of the personality, which has many functions such as perception, memory, thinking, and defense. These ego functions develop naturally as a normal part of our development and they are necessary for adaptation, survival, and growth. Ultimately these functions contribute to our maturation along developmental stages. While it's beyond the scope of this chapter to delve into the various stages of development famously described by researchers and psychologists like Freud, Mahler, and Eriksen, suffice it to say that your ego developed from your life experiences, and its **principal goal is to protect you and ensure your survival**.

From the critical moment a child begins to sense that she is separate from her mother the process of programming begins. Unless we had super attentive, responsive loving parents, for most of us, this is also when a state of *dis*-ease is entered.

Your Programmed Self-Image

Who do you think you are?

How you perceive yourself is largely based on how you were programmed to see yourself. From the time you were born the interactions you had with the outside world shaped your sense of self. If you had highly conscious, emotionally aware parents and caretakers who saw you as a being full of potential, possessing innate gifts, and with a unique mission to express in the world, then your current self-description may be 'accurate.' But if you're like most people, then who you think you are is just a *fraction* of your potential self, at best. And if you're like me, before you consciously define it, your self-concept may be totally false!

Neurobiologists tell us that during the first six to seven years of a child's life the brain is in a mostly passive, receptive mode. In this early state of development, the brain receives information passively — without analyzing or reasoning. Those are functions of the higher brain centers, which develop later in childhood all the way through to early adulthood. The electrical brain wave patterns of young children seven and under are dominated by delta and theta brain waves, which are the brain waves associated with sleep, dreaming and deep trance states. These types of brain patterns mean that the subconscious mind records everything — and I do mean *everything* — like a surveillance camera running 24/7.

During this impressionable state you learn and adopt beliefs about yourself that impact your self-esteem, self-confidence, and self-efficacy, which is your belief in your ability to succeed in mastering tasks. How crazy is it that your attitudes about your identity, biases about your place in the world, and assumptions about your ability to succeed in life, were programmed into your subconscious mind at a time when you were in a hypnotic state; unable to think for yourself?!

This means that your knucklehead brother, socially deprived nanny, or conformity-inspired preschool teacher had a dramatic impact on who you think you are. For example hearing an older sibling, parent, or teacher frequently berate you or belittle you can make you feel that you are inherently bad, wrong or stupid. You didn't have mature brain circuits which would allow you to challenge or dispute their judgements of you. Instead, without knowing it you internalized, their beliefs about you. And some of those beliefs may still be lingering in your subconscious mind holding you back from feeling confident to pursue your dreams or live life on your terms.

God bless the parents, teachers, coaches, and family members who were positive, encouraging, and uplifting in our early lives! At least some of their influence may have helped you know yourself to be the unique and precious treasure that you are.

What you see in yourself now — and your thoughts about who you are in relationship to your outside reality — is a function of the beliefs and assumptions stored in your subconscious mind. I cannot stress this enough. So many of my patients and clients over the years were astounded to realize that much of what you see in yourself today is based on the beliefs that were formed (or accepted) in the past. Despite your advanced degrees, street smarts or intense learning you've done searching the Internet and reading self-help books, your intellect can sometimes be insufficient when it comes to overcoming programmed biases. So if you feel that some of the hidden beliefs may be holding you back from changing your life, achieving your goals, or feeling happy, take heart. This does not need to be the case going forward.

Like debugging a computer of viruses, all limiting beliefs and mental concepts hidden in your mind that are not in line with a life of joy and harmony will be removed.

How childhood programming affects adult behavior

The way that information is stored in our subconscious mind is not haphazard. During childhood, all of the data our brain receives from the outside world is filed into two main categories: things that create more safety and/or pleasure vs. things that cause pain, or threat of injury. This categorization process will continue to show up throughout life, causing us to gravitate toward things that make us feel safe and loved while rejecting or recoiling from things that produce fear and pain. This is survival based programming. We all have it.

It's amazing to realize that love and fear, the two dominant drivers of our present thoughts and behaviors, were already being distinguished early on in our infancy and childhood. Based on our past experiences, our brains registered some people or circumstances potential threats to our survival and labeled some people or things as favorable, desirable and worth pursuing because they brought us comfort or safety. Much of this happened before our rational brain centers were in use, so some of those associations are not even logical. As such, it should be no surprise that we often find an inner four year old running our present life and relationships in some way!

The subconscious mind of the child who heard that she must "eat everything on the plate" because of starving children around the world records the message that *there is not enough food for everyone.* This record is filed away in the back of the mind as a belief in scarcity. The scarcity consciousness of the child you were decades ago may now cause you to eat more food than you need simply because it's on your plate. Without conscious thought, you may feel compelled to take it all in, or to accept the food offered to you because, it could be worse, you could have no food at all. This is how overeaters and hoarders are often bred.

Another example, is the subconscious mind of the child whose cries were not attended to regularly or in a consistent, timely manner. He or she may have recorded a belief that people are unreliable or that they themselves are not worthy of love and attention. In adult relationships, these beliefs may then drive irrational behaviors of unnecessary clinginess on one hand or extreme suspicion and sabotage on the other. This is how loners and frequently-abandoned people may develop.

Many of us also learned to distrust our own feelings and insights. We might have come up with new ways to do something or solve problems, only for our innovation to be deemed silly, impossible or too time consuming. This is one way that we habitually reject our first impulses or intuition in favor of popular theory or the majority vote.

One of the miraculous discoveries made during my recovery process was learning that I can trust my first flash of insight. Whether it relates to finding my way to a new place when I *think* I may be lost to making a good decision for a client, my intuition and heart-sense are rarely wrong. I have learned over time that I do not need to revise and tweak my work to perfection. I can trust that the inspiration that pours forth during my work is right on target, and just what is needed for the present moment and all involved.

When you look at your own life can you see if there is a pattern of over-thinking your decisions instead of trusting your first mind, your first heart-based impression? Are there automatic patterns of rejection or attraction that seem to drive you or move you that aren't totally aligned with your heart's desires?

The good news is that we can go in and change these old, useless, and often harmful messages that were implanted earlier in life. We can then install healthier mindsets which will become the guiding information to consciously co-create the life we desire to live in the NOW.

How subconscious memories impact present biology & behavior

It's not only the experiences we have in childhood that can impact our present behaviors and self-image. The subconscious mind will also record messages about what you're experiencing in the present or recent past, like the painful heartbreak you suffered last year, the fear and anger you harbor about losing your job six months ago, and the stress you feel after having served in a war. We store the energy and information of *all* experiences in our subconscious minds and in the cells of our bodies.

What do these stored experiences feel like? The energetic memory of abandonment or heartache may deplete your brain's stores of serotonin — the natural feel good chemical —

resulting in lowered energy and low moods. Suffering a major defeat or disappointment at work can lodge itself in your muscles causing you to feel weak and achy. The information you may have stored about your unworthiness of abundance, and the accompanying feeling of not deserving a better paying job holds you in a fearful pattern of upset stomach, insomnia, and worry.

Our beliefs and perceptions also influence our physical health — right down to turning on cancer genes. Even geneticists agree that over 65% of disease is NOT determined by the DNA in our genes as previously thought. The study of epigenetics tells us that our environment and perception about what's going on around us, can directly impact our gene expression. *Our own thoughts and beliefs can influence our physical health.*

Unless we become conscious and aware, our survival instincts will continue to run our lives based on old programming. While it may seem overwhelming to think of all the stored data in your mind — and cells — the most important thing is for you to become aware that you can change all of that right NOW — in an instant. You have the power to decide the life you want to live, the person you want to be, and the feelings you want to have. *You can change right now.*

The Cornerstone Process will lead you step-by-step back to a natural state of calmness, confidence, and clarity where you can transform your life and all the situations in it. This process arms you with new insights to guide you back to your own state of wholeness and perfect intelligence.

How resilience plays a role in our wellbeing

If balance and wholeness represent our natural state why do some people bounce back easier than others? Why do some rise after defeat rather than wither into obscurity? How is it that some people can adapt to stressful situations better than others?

Personally, I've been curious to understand why do siblings born into the same families with similar exposures sometimes grow into completely opposite adults. Example, why do some victims of abuse become abusers as adults while their siblings, who also suffered abuse, become rescuers? What makes one child respond to a demanding, critical parent with perfectionism while another withdraws and becomes an underachiever? It turns out that inborn and inherited qualities of personality also influence how we perceive, interpret, and label our experiences.

Once we've revealed the programmed version of you, the elements that make up your earth-based self-identity, or the m'ego, as I like to call it, we can explore the elements of your self-identity that transcend the life experiences and programming you experienced since your birth. Throughout this book you will learn how to reinterpret, re-label and re-empower yourself to become more resilient and robust than ever before.

Now let's explore the aspects of your personality that may come pre-installed at birth.

What influences temperament and personality

There is a fair amount of debate about how much of our personality is determined by genetics and how much is impacted by our environment, including the way we were brought up. The nature vs. nurture vs. environment argument is a heated one, and rather than split hairs on the precise influence determined from large population studies, I invite you to look at yourself, and your family and close friends to see what is true based on your observation. You're actually a pretty good scientist, so don't shy away from coming up with conclusions based on the following sections.

The world is mistakenly set up based on a single approach to success, happiness, and fulfillment, when the truth is that because each of us is different there are *multiple* ways to live, work, and play that will lead to personal happiness and well-being. The 'multi-norm' philosophy respects our individuality and encourages us to accept that each of us is different and the world is better for it.

Understanding and accepting who you are can help eliminate tons of waste in many areas. We waste energy, time, and relationships due to misunderstandings and arguments, which could be prevented if we had more intelligence and understanding about our true nature, traits, and talents. And if we accept and respect the innate talents, traits and nature of others we will live with more harmony and compassion.

I know that many of my days and nights were wasted as I hid from the world, withdrew from activities, and pushed myself to achieve goals that ended up being useless to me and ultimately drained me. Now that I've spent years getting to know and accept the parts of me that came with the package, I live in more peace and harmony. I embrace my strengths and use them to my advantage. I can even accept my flaws and minimize their destructive power.

So let's explore some well researched systems that may help you identify core traits that make up your personality in undeniable ways.

The 5 Earth Elements — Your Natural Energy Imprint

For most of us, unless there was significant birth trauma or a problematic pregnancy, we are born in a state of wellbeing. All of our organ systems are poised for a perfect life, full of the ability to weather the various storms of life with resilience and grace. We are born with the natural tendency to thrive.

Just as children bounce back after sickness and surgery, we adults can do the same. The innate biological wisdom for homeostasis and recovery can be tapped right now to recover from illness, injury and disease. Just as children change activities, hobbies and 'best friends' with ease, we adults can change the course of our lives from humdrum to rapturous with little resistance. In fact, we can be dancing, frolicking and playing for decades to come.

The ancient Chinese and Taoist concepts of the 5 elements along with acupuncture and qigong have truly been a blessing in my life to help understand our personal and Universal energy. According to Taoist philosophy, as espoused by Traditional Chinese Medicine (TCM), we can renew our vitality and return to a natural state of wholeness and wellness when we live in accordance with our true nature and the flow of nature around us. We each carry an energetic blueprint for optimal wellbeing, happiness and success. This energy imprint dictates how our body, mind and heart naturally integrate to make us whole beings for a long, healthy life of active, vibrant living.

According to the TCM system, when we allow our natural energy signature to inform and guide our lifestyle we can live wholly, fully and resiliently — naturally. In the Chinese medical view, the human body-mind is like a microcosm correlated to the macrocosm of the universe or nature. Just as nature recovers after hurricanes, droughts and volcanic eruptions, when we experience setbacks or bumps on our journey through life, they need not derail us entirely. Our own natural forces can bring us back to wellness and set us back on the course to optimal wellbeing and the pursuit of our highest ideals.

Beyond my training in Chinese medicine and acupuncture, and my education in medicine and surgery, I have personally experienced the transformation and healing that springs from becoming aware of who I am and how I am constructed from an elemental perspective. By aligning my business, family and social life with my natural inclinations, personality, values and energetic influences I have become free of lifelong depression, stifling anxiety and a persistent lack of love and self-acceptance. I find it incredibly helpful to be aware of the energetic influences you were born with.

To explore your elemental influences, you can gain valuable insight by taking the free Vitality Test, developed by my colleague Nick Haines of the Five Institute. Your results will teach you which of the 5 Chinese elements is your dominant type — Water, Wood, Metal, Earth, Fire.

By taking the Vitality Test you increase your self-awareness and learn more about the influences which drive and motivate you, what makes you naturally brilliant and potentially vulnerable to stress. There is something reassuring and life-affirming to understand that your personality traits and emotional tendencies are better understood in the context of your whole, natural composition. We truly are part of the entire earth ecosystem.

Trying to deny or reject the parts of us that are deeply ingrained within our makeup creates stress and confusion.

In my 5 Elements profile results I see that I have almost equal influences from the Wood and Water elements, with Fire coming in a close third position. The Wood and Fire influences have inspired me to create new businesses, jump into exciting ventures, move to foreign countries and take the lead on campaigns which have brought me a sense of fulfillment. However, at times when I have become overly controlling, rigid or obsessive, those Elements were used up and I was left burnt out. Not honoring my body's energy rhythm and flow caused me to struggle with terrible muscle stiffness and neck tension, insomnia and irritability and and anxiety — all due to Wood Energy imbalances.

By taking a closer look at my Energy imprint, my old habits and past disappointments I became conscious of patterns in my body, mind and environment that regularly preceded irritable and stormy moods. These insights helped me to learn how to prevent problems from occurring by anticipating the possibility of overextending myself and judiciously taking on only what I could reasonably handle with adequate self-care time. I also became better at heeding the warning signs of an impending breakdown my body gave me.

My personality is naturally geared toward starting new ventures and entrepreneurship, a common trait for people with a lot of Wood energy in their profile. When a project is up and running or I have mastered a given subject I often lose interest and start looking for new challenges. One business mentor told me that I've got "shiny penny syndrome" because I jump onto the next big sparkly idea that hits my awareness. During my teens I heard that being a dilettante, someone with multiple interests, was considered a bad thing. I was labeled a "Jane of all trades, master of none", which made me feel terrible for being passionate about a huge variety of subjects.

Knowing this is not some defect or inability to focus, I've taken this knowledge and planned my business life accordingly. I now allow myself to explore and dig into new exciting ideas while maintaining my focus and following through on my projects.

I have since taught clients and workshop attendees around the world these processes, and they like me, have found the ability to recover from illness, to heal themselves, and achieve their goals with stress-less ease. When we accept and embrace who we are, forgive our past mistakes and commit to living authentically in tune with the natural flow of energy, we can recover from breakdowns, burnout and breakups as well as bounce back from disease and devastation. Most importantly, we can reclaim our lives and move into a whole new paradigm of existence.

A client of mine, Diane, discovered that her lifetime tendency to look after, support and encourage others reflects her dominant Earth Energy type. By becoming aware of her frequent tendency to self-sacrifice to the point of exhaustion alternating with subsequent periods of using food to calm and soothe herself she was able to nip destructive overeating cycles in the bud. Further, by learning and practicing the Attunement Meditation, explained in Part 3 of the book, Diane became much more in tune with her body's various messages and signals and was able to self-diagnose her own breast and colon cancers!

The various lessons she learned, that you will read about in this book, empowered Diane to take her newfound, clean bill of health in stride as she reprioritized her own wellbeing and health. She is taking her momentum and positivity forward to enjoy her the rest of her life as a cancer-free, vivacious woman!

So be sure to take the free Vitality Test to find out which of the 5 elements influence you the most so you can see how they impact your ability to love, accept and express your Authentic Self.

Nature, Astrology, and the Authentic You

Have you explored what your astrological sign has to say about your personality, or how it influences your lifelong ambitions? I was born on November 9 and my sun sign is Scorpio. Up until the year 2000 I didn't believe in astrology one bit. When I met, Alexander, someone who has come to be one of my most treasured friends in this life, I discovered that so much of my personality and preferences could be explained by casting my birth chart. Later, with the exploration of Indian or Vedic astrology I became convinced that I could become even more confident and self-assured by looking into my nature as influenced by celestial bodies.

Now I'm not suggesting that your daily horoscope could be the answer to all of your existential angst. However, recognizing that a part of who you are is linked to the placement and movement of the moon, stars, and planets in the heavens shows that you're more than flesh, blood, and bundled up neuroses. You're also connected to the celestial bodies and their energies and position at the time of your birth. To see how the transit of the planets through your astrological chart influences your moods, energy levels, and achievement cycles, can be profound.

I am no expert on any form of astrology, nor do I follow the transit of planets through my chart on a regular basis, but I will say that having a few readings has helped me better understand, accept, and love myself. So keep an open mind here.

Of course, even though we may have the same Sun sign, we are so different in our mix and expression of our nature. There's no other person on the planet like you. And there is no other person like me. And respecting your natural rhythms and preferences is the key to feeling confident and comfortable in your own skin.

A farmer wouldn't dream of planting tomatoes in winter. He instead respects the season and cycle of time he takes to planting based on the weather and environment, while cultivating the soil for maximal fertile growth. We are not separate from nature, *we are a part of it*. As a human being we're a self-contained energy system, just as the earth herself is. As we are individuals who make up families, communities, nations, and the entire earth family, we are on a planet that is also a small system that is part of a larger system. We are part of the solar system, the universe and the multiverse.

So many of us suffer because we are not living in alignment with our true nature. This means we are out of harmony with ourselves from the deepest levels and we're not in harmony with Mother Earth either.

My life journey, professional career, and personal study, have shown me that from the beginning of time, before societal structure and religions drove humankind into hiding or conformity, our natural expressiveness allowed people to thrive in various cultures and societies. It was assumed that we each have a part to play in the intricately designed, delicately interwoven tapestry of life.

Coming out of my near-death-like experience I felt so optimistic, hopeful, and curious about what life would be like living on my own terms. It was always easy to see clearly how and what *others* could do to feel more ease by not fighting who they are. But for me, knowing and accepting myself seemed hard because of longstanding habits, cultural programming, and the brainwashing I had endured in childhood, my peer groups, and with the media. The assumption that we are perfect and capable of thriving while living in harmony with our basic nature seems radical at first. We fear that by rejecting societal norms we'll be cast out, rejected, and ridiculed.

By playing it safe we cram ourselves into molds, holes, and roles that don't fit us or allow us to grow to be who we really want to be.

I hope you can see now why it is my passion to help you reawaken this innate wisdom, which is contained in your DNA, your spirit, and your heart. This wisdom points to a future where you'll live powerfully and passionately with yourself, the earth, and your environment. Knowing yourself and what you need to thrive in all areas of life will set you free. You can take this information to transform your mindset, lifestyle, career, and relationships so that you flourish.

If we accept that we are all naturally different, and stop trying to fit everybody (and ourself) into a narrow and artificial model, we take away enormous pain and wasted time. Instead of curing, repressing, and denying a talent that doesn't fit into a single-norm model, we can look for ways to express our talent in a positive manner. This would enrich our lives enormously in *every* way. Ultimately, happy, well-adjusted individuals benefit society.

Living in accordance with your nature does three important things:

1. It builds up your confidence. Consequently you're able to go after your goals.

2. It promotes free self-expression. Lack of suppression leads to wholeness, vitality and good health.

3. By not denying and fighting yourself, you experience joy, instead of guilt or anxiety. This leads to well-being, goodwill and a willingness to cooperate with other people. You don't envy others because you're happy in your own skin. Overall, whatever the various tasks you perform in life, you become a pillar of society. You serve life in a constructive manner.

Summary Insights & Questions to Consider Regarding Your Personality

1. Who are you? Self-awareness, the first step of becoming who you really are, is at the heart of true self-love.

2. Are there any family beliefs, myths or sayings that still impact you today?

3. Which illnesses or health conditions impact many people in your family?

4. What in your life, body, or thoughts are you judging?

5. Are you "shoulding" or "oughting"?

6. Are you acting or reacting to life, situations, and ideals?

Now that we have identified how certain aspects of your personality were programmed or inherited let's explore how the blend of these traits and reactionary programs are influencing you today. In the next chapter we will start to move into the empowered territory of consciously aligning with our best self.

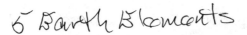

5 Barth Bloments

2

How the Programmed You and Real You Appear In Your Life

"You can't get where you want to be without knowing where you are."

Strength-Based Psychology: What's Right About You?

About 16 years ago I was introduced to the wonderful world of positive psychology. I love it because this branch of psychology shifts the focus from what's wrong in humans to the positive qualities that help us flourish and thrive. Being a bit of a nerd, I love that, as a science, positive psychology has validated a number of surveys, questionnaires, and most importantly, practices which have been proven to lead to greater well-being and life satisfaction.

If I were working with you one-on-one, as a starting point, we'd identify your strengths; the qualities that allow you to perform well or at your personal best. I know that if we use your strengths and talents, to organize your *whole* life, including your work, play, and relationships in such a way that you utilize your strengths regularly, you'll experience greater life satisfaction. Also, using strengths in times of adversity or conflict can help you better cope with the situation and find a resolution.

Your Values In Action

For over a decade the VIA (Values in Action) Institute has studied and assisted people in identifying and using strengths. Their research has uncovered the twenty-four character traits ı in human beings across cultures and time, which are universal to the human experience. These strengths are values you embody that help make you who you are — they are within you and are generally stable over time. It's widely recognized that focusing and building on your strengths, rather than your weaknesses, can make for a happier, meaningful life in which you are engaged and living more optimally.

The VIA Institute offers free web-based assessment tools to discover your strengths. You can take the VIA for free here: www.VIACharacter.org.

Below are the twenty-four traits they've defined.

1. **Creativity (originality, ingenuity):** Thinking of novel and productive ways to conceptualize and do things.

2. **Curiosity (interest, novelty-seeking, openness to experience):** Taking an interest in ongoing experience for its own sake; exploring and discovering.

3. **Open-mindedness (judgment, critical thinking):** Thinking things through and examining them from all sides; weighing all evidence fairly.

4. **Love of learning:** Mastering new skills, topics, and bodies of knowledge, whether on your own or in formal settings.

5. **Perspective (wisdom):** Being able to provide wise counsel to others; having ways of looking at the world that make sense to oneself and to other people.

6. **Bravery (valor):** Not shrinking from threat, challenge, difficulty, or pain; acting on convictions even if unpopular.

7. **Persistence (perseverance, industriousness):** Finishing what one starts; persisting in a course of action in spite of obstacles.

8. **Integrity (authenticity, honesty):** Presenting oneself in a genuine way; taking responsibility for one's feelings and actions.

9. **Vitality (zest, enthusiasm, vigor, energy):** Approaching life with excitement and energy; feeling alive and activated.

10. **Love:** Valuing close relations with others, in particular those in which sharing and caring are reciprocated.

11. **Kindness (generosity, nurturance, care, compassion, altruistic love, "niceness"):** Doing favors and good deeds for others.

12. **Social intelligence (emotional intelligence, personal intelligence):** Being aware of the motives and feelings of other people and oneself.

13. **Citizenship (social responsibility, loyalty, teamwork):** Working well as a member of a group or team; being loyal to the group.

14. **Fairness:** Treating all people the same according to notions of fairness and justice; not letting personal feelings bias decisions about others.

15. **Leadership:** Encouraging a group of which one is a member to get things done and at the same maintain time good relations within the group.

16. **Forgiveness and mercy:** Forgiving those who have done wrong; accepting the shortcomings of others; giving people a second chance; not being vengeful.

17. **Humility / Modesty:** Letting one's accomplishments speak for themselves; not regarding oneself as more special than one is.

18. **Prudence:** Being careful about one's choices; not taking undue risks; not saying or doing things that might later be regretted.

19. **Self-regulation (self-control):** Regulating what one feels and does; being disciplined; controlling one's appetites and emotions.

20. **Appreciation of beauty and excellence (awe, wonder, elevation):** Appreciating beauty, excellence, and/or skilled performance in various domains of life.

21. **Gratitude:** Being aware of and thankful for the good things that happen; taking time to express thanks.

22. **Hope (optimism, future-mindedness, future orientation):** Expecting the best in the future and working to achieve it.

23. **Humor (playfulness):** Liking to laugh and tease; bringing smiles to other people; seeing the light side.

24. **Spirituality (religiousness, faith, purpose):** Having coherent beliefs about the higher purpose, the meaning of life, and the meaning of the universe.

Once you've taken the VIA survey to identify your top five strengths, I suggest that you utilize two of your strengths in ways you've not done before, every day for a two-week period and journal about your experience.

Studies have shown that after completing this exercise, participants were more likely to report harmonious passion and engagement in life. What's exciting is that this passion was associated with improved well-being and satisfaction with life. By just being more of who you already are, you'll experience more joy. Cool, right?

Just imagine the benefits you would enjoy if you consistently utilized these strengths.

If you have completed the Values in Action (VIA) survey to determine your signature strengths and personality drivers, how does it feel to see your most positive qualities staring back at you in black and white? Can you get a better sense of how these elements of your personality have shaped your decisions, your outlook on life, and your accomplishments so far? Do you recognize a hint of truth about who you really are?

For the most part, these are the qualities that reveal parts of your true nature, despite how they may be denied, hidden at times, or not fully and clearly seen. Shining a light on the ways that various elements of your personality actually show up in daily life is a critical part in laying your cornerstone of self-love and unconditional self-acceptance. In fact, in times past, before placing a cornerstone, people often performed a ceremony, which included burying special objects, written documents, or other personal elements beneath the foundation stone. Then the building was constructed upon those objects. It's the same with building your personal temple.

The ingredients and personal attributes of your Authentic Self, your divine traits, and innate talents have been buried under the life experiences you've had and stored within the body you inhabit today. By engaging in this conscious process of identifying and uncovering your core essence, you can reawaken the original you, and rebuild your life, your body, and your relationships in alignment with your true spiritual self.

So let's take a look at the practical side of how your strengths and innate positive qualities show up in real life today.

Your Peak Experiences — Your Values and Strengths In Action

I'd like you to think about your most positive experience that you can remember. Think of a time when you felt blissful, powerful, proud, and full of energy. Think of a time when you felt like you were totally in the zone, at your highest mood.

You may have been onstage performing music or dance. Perhaps you were volunteering in the community. Peak experiences are usually those where you felt completely absorbed in what you were doing, as if you were lost in the action. You could've been with other people or totally alone. Maybe you were doing a sports activity, gardening, hiking, or watching the sun set. It could have been the first time you held your baby. Bring one such magical moment to mind. We will explore how this peak experience gives you clues to your hidden talents or core values.

In the 1950's, the American psychologist, Abraham Maslow, studied people who were considered exceptional or 'super human.' Rather than focusing on the troubled mind in psychology, he was curious to understand the make up of highly functional, compassionate and thriving people. Through his research he began to identify people who were said to have mystical experiences or magical moments. He summarized his findings and described what we now refer to as the peak experience, which includes an oceanic feeling of ecstasy. This includes feelings of limitless horizons, being opened up to a grand vision, a sense of simultaneously being more powerful and more helpless than one ever was, experiencing great ecstasy, wonder and awe, and the sensation of a loss of time and space. As one comes out of these peak experiences, Maslow documented that many people had a strong conviction that something extremely important and valuable had happened.

The people he studied were considered extraordinary, people we might call high achievers or peak performers. They were not, however, considered spiritual or particularly religious people. Yet, he noticed that the magical moments they described often included the same words as spoken by Mother Theresa, Meister Eckhart and other famous mystics. Maslow's studies revealed that many of the peak experiences were triggered by being in nature, being overtaken by music, by love, and even during childbirth. And when stripped of the religious meaning that one normally thinks of, he also found that the experience of perfection — in athletics, performing music or in natural childbirth — could induce a peak experience.

Sometimes, part of the experience involves a sense that things just *flowed* in the right rhythm and energy. You may have heard how Eastern philosophy calls this being one with the Tao. Modern psychologists refer to it as being in the state of flow.

Renowned American-Hungarian psychologist, Mihaly Csikszentmihalyi, defined flow as a highly focused mental state in which people are "so involved in an activity that nothing else seems to matter; the experience is so enjoyable that people will continue to do it even at great cost, for the sheer sake of doing it." He identified a number of different elements involved in achieving or triggering flow:

- There are **clear goals** every step of the way.

- There is **immediate feedback** to your actions.

- There is a **balance between challenges and skills.**

- **Action and awareness** are **merged**.

- **Distractions are excluded** from consciousness.

- There is **no worry of failure.**

- **Self-consciousness disappears.**

- The sense of **time becomes distorted.**

- The **activity becomes an end in itself.**

Peak experiences and the flow state

The point of looking at one of your peak experiences is to teach, or remind yourself, that you can lose sight of the preprogrammed version of yourself, when you become *one* with a task, nature, or pure love. That's when you can transcend the m'ego and return to living in alignment with your Authentic Self. The state of flow is what makes most people feel like their life is worth living. The desire to return to a state of flow is what fuels many musicians, athletes, entrepreneurs, artists, adventurers, and other creative types in their work.

For ordinary people living ordinary lives, it's the experience of flow that gives us a sense of having a place in the universe that matters. I believe that the more we orient our lives around the natural ability to enter the state of flow the greater our sense of happiness, fulfillment, and harmony. From that elevated standpoint we can begin to have an extraordinary impact in the world around us. Positive psychology research has shown us time and again that this is possible. There are even 'flow hackers' like Steven Kotler and Jamie Wheal who have built companies, written books, created online courses and even launched adult flow-camps to bring more rigor to the science of creating more flow in life. The popularity of flow hacking is justified: when we know what lights us up and brings us into a state of elevated consciousness, we are in a position to use more of our life force energy and human potential to heal, thrive, achieve, love and be a greater contribution to the world at large.

In my own life, I've proven to myself over and over, that when I align my work, play, relationships, and environments in a way that fosters the flow state, I flourish. I thrive best when I'm using my skills and passions in a way that is meaningful to others and personally fulfilling. It's not one or the other for me and other flow hackers.

In the flow state I lose sense of time and self, I feel more creative, powerful, and more like 'me.' I feel merged with a divine state of consciousness and bliss. I have consciously architected my life to allow myself to enter the flow state frequently — almost on a daily basis — through creative brainstorming, working with clients, performing on stage, meditating, dancing, and listening to or singing music. It goes without saying that sexual intimacy provides a flow-filled experience, too!

I invite you to explore how during a peak experience, as you move beyond the impression of being small or limited, you gain access to your greater potential for self-expression. This opens you up to higher states of consciousness, which permit more and more of the authentic you to emerge. Reliving or describing the peak experience documents how utilizing your inborn strengths, your developed talents and your personal drive allows you to find joy in living.

Take thirty minutes or so to get in touch with the memory of a few peak experiences you've had. Write one or several down here or in a journal. Do this now as we will come back to it in another exercise in this chapter.

My Peak Experiences

_____

_____

_____

_____

_____

_____

_____

_____

_____

_____

_____

_____

_____

_____

_____

_____

_____

To continue our self-discover journey, it's time to uncover another critical element of the Authentic Self, your spiritual DNA.

Your Spiritual DNA: Virtues, Values, Dreams and Desires

Consider your spiritual DNA as the blueprint for constructing your authentic life. Just as basic templates exist for the construction of houses, paper dolls, and clothing, it's how we creatively express our tastes and desires through color, texture, and fabrics that adds our unique signature to the final products.

Your passions, your dreams, and your desires are the additional self-expression materials and accessories which adorn you and your life. The blueprint for your Authentic Self was present before your birth, and how you express yourself in how you add flair and individuality to the living temple of your Authentic Self. Your dreams, fantasies and wishes are also the impulses that drive you or (nag you!) to take action.

Your spiritual DNA represents the wishes from your higher self, spirit, or your soul; and they make up the architectural design for how your life *could* be constructed to reach your highest potential. You always have free will. You don't have to follow the spiritual blueprint if you choose not to. Though most find that living contrary to what their soul is calling for brings up a great deal of suffering.

For the last few years I have attended a yearly spiritual retreat hosted by the Sisters of the Brahma Kumaris. This special retreat is led by Sister Jenna, host of the America Meditating radio show and Founder of the Brahma Kumaris Meditation Museums in the Washington, DC area. At the start of the retreat we explore two aspects of our human experience: one is Soul Awareness and the other Body Awareness. I love the way they explain that since our soul's nature is pure, we can easily see when our spiritual DNA is active because we will experience or embody traits of the soul. For example, when you are aligned with your soul, you feel comfortable inside no matter what happens, your heart is open and loving, you love yourself, you attract beauty, your confidence and self-respect soars, your life is meaningful, peace is your religion and spirituality becomes second nature.

On the other hand, when we are dominated by the experience-focused body awareness, we feel anxious and uptight, we are grumpy and short tempered, we are out of harmony with our body, we are motivated by short-term desires, we criticize and find fault with everyone, our happiness doesn't last and we have low self-esteem and a lot of ego.

Because our true nature is spiritual, our soul will naturally nudge us toward returning to the true self and our best life path, if we become sensitive to it and follow it's guidance. One way that I've found that my soul has led me back to my spiritual core is by looking at the desires, deep urges and longings that come up in life. Not the whimsical, hedonistic or self-centered ones. I'm talking about the impulses that inspire awe, wonder and humility. The deep motivations, driven by the soul's virtues, values and desires are worth paying special attention to. When we tune into these virtues, and the activities which allow us to experience and express them, we activate the source code for an extraordinary life of meaning and purpose.

Virtues

21 Soul virtues are part of your spiritual DNA

The Brahma Kumaris also teach that there are 21 Virtues of the Soul that shine through when we allow our true nature to lead us. While we may not express our highest virtues all of the time, they are inherent in our soul programming, and they can be cultivated. As if encoded in our spiritual DNA we will find that living in alignment with the true self, in connection with your spirit inspires you to express these virtues.

Examples of the 21 Virtues include: Brotherhood, where you recognize your connection to humanity; Contentment, realizing that looking at your past achievements you really have everything you need; Compassion helps you perceive needs without judging and send out good wishes. Courage, Delicacy, Detachment, Discernment, Discipline, on to Enthusiasm, Faith and Friendship comprise other soul Virtues.

It's easy to see that when you love and accept your Authentic Self, the part of you that comes from purity and wholeness, these virtues seem obvious. From Happiness, Harmony, Humility, Patience, Responsibility, Self-Confidence, Simplicity, Spontaneity, Tolerance and Wisdom you'll enjoy a light-filled life when you live in alignment with soul qualities.

Reading through these last two paragraphs, can you sense that these virtuous qualities are naturally embodied by the people we typically consider holy, wise, 'woke' or humble?

When you think of His Holiness the Dalai Lama, Mother Theresa, Thích Nhất Hạnh, Martin Luther King, Jr., Gandhi, Nelson Mandela, Sister Jenna, and others, you see that they are the epitome of Soul Virtues. You also have the inborn capacity to radiate these qualities with you live as your Authentic Self and cultivate the presence of your soul.

Desires and dreams

Where there is burning desire there is the soul's deepest wish.

Another way to discover your unique soul qualities is by exploring the dreams and desires you long to achieve. Are there dreams or wishes that you've felt most of your life, or for a long time, that you've pushed away and instead pursued more 'practical' activities? What would you like to change or experience now or in the next twelve months that would make you feel happy and successful? What is your greatest dream or vision for your life?

Do you desire more abundance, a home full of family and friends, another career? Is there an activity or skill you'd like to acquire that would bring you a sense of fulfillment and joy?

What would you do if money and time were of no concern? Is there something that you would even *pay* to do or experience if you were a billionaire?

What would you do, where would you live, who would you be with, and how would you act, if you had no fear of judgment or criticism from anyone?

I believe our dreams and desires may provide clues to the hidden ideals of our soul. Beyond the common wishes for more creature comforts that nearly everyone wants, we each feel deep impulses for how we want to be, exist, play, and love in our lives. Some of us have a wishful image of the life we want to lead that comes from a place beyond our flesh, blood, and mental programming.

When we get back in touch with our dreams and desires we can reignite the fire of passion within. This can fuel our ability to create new goals to live an awakened life of mutual success, cooperation, and achievement. When we accept these dreams as evidence of our innate worth and potential ability to make valuable contribution, we can believe in ourselves again.

One dream of mine that I've denied and downplayed is to sing soulful music on stages, on albums, online — basically anywhere! While studying at university I sang in an R&B group. I never imagined myself to be some upcoming pop star, the lyrics I wrote to our songs were always a bit too deep for our producers' tastes. Instead I longed to express profound emotion, love and joy through music.

People said I was an old soul, and singing spiritual jazz at my age wasn't commercially interesting to them. Based on the world I knew at that time, there just wasn't a place for a singer like me, other than the church. And since I wasn't willing to mold myself into a pop package, I let the pursuit of music fall by the wayside. But only for a while. I did play trumpet and sing in our church choir for a few years.

The desire and urge to write and sing and perform came back again and again through my life, often to save me from drowning in depression. While I was consumed with a disheartening amount of studying and feeling inadequate in medical school, it was playing piano and singing jazz standards that lifted my moods. When I was running my wellness institute and working on TV every day, it was the evenings and weekends spent singing and composing songs that balanced my moods.

All the way up to 2019, the urge and desire to sing has persisted, but I didn't give it much thought. Once again, the idea that there are more important and serious things to concern myself with have taken priority. But over the last two years it has become such a strong force that I could no longer deny music a place in my life — beyond the shower or the car!

I have even heard the call to sing from the outside world. To further nudge me along the universe has sent messages from people who've heard little snippets of my music online asking when and where they could get more. Even my inner circle of friends and supporters have requested that I sing at their events.

I have realized that previously I considered my singing to be an ego-based pursuit. After all, why do most people record albums or perform live? In my mind, it was to become famous or rich. And since I've been feeling the call to evolve my soul and focus on spiritual growth, singing didn't seem to fit. That is until the calls from inside and outside were so strong, and the signs so compelling that I stopped resisting. I finally got the message that the healing power of music and my voice are not for me alone.

I've been blessed with connections to other musicians who have a similar spiritual focus and who are touching lives around the world through Conscious Music, including the beautiful souls of Paul Luftenegger and Kristin Hoffmann. Both of these amazing singer, songwriter, musicians were with me at the spiritual retreats with Sister Jenna that I mentioned earlier. And their concerts stirred my soul so immensely I longed to share my voice in celebration of life and creativity.

I had the pleasure of traveling with Kristin in Peru on another retreat and with Paul in India. Experiencing the effect of the loving way they honor their voices, their creative flow and their connection to the Divine Source of life has shown me a new path. Music is a universal language of healing, peace and connection.

After our trip to India in 2018, Paul shared a vision he had. In addition to writing and performing soul stirring songs, Paul is also a powerful spiritual medium! He told me that he saw music and performance playing a bigger role in my life than I was currently allowing. I can't deny it either, Paul was merely confirming something that God told me earlier.

While perched high atop Mount Abu in India, silently connecting to the divine Light within, I was eagerly anticipating some spiritual insight from God to arrive. After all, that's why one goes to an ashram in India, right? As I sat in meditation I heard a clear voice telling me I was to start a record label. At first I was like "Say what??? I asked for a spiritual wisdom download, and you tell me this???"

I've learned, however, that when the Divine speaks, it's best for me to listen. Sooner or later the signs get more glaring as the outside voices become more prominent and persistent. It's as if our soul conspires with the Divine and the whole Universe to nudge us — or flat out push us! — into our soul's true calling. At the end of 2018 I said 'Yes' and I decided to welcome music into my life in whatever way is best.

Within days I started waking up most mornings around 4 or 5am with songs running in my head. New music tunes or lyrics were flowing through my consciousness, so I grabbed my iPad and whispered the melodies into the voice recorder to avoid forgetting them. This has made me consider that maybe music is a part of my soul's journey to wholeness and connection, installed in this vessel for a purpose beyond my ego's comprehension. Rather than control or deny it, why not let it flow? Old habits die hard apparently.

We've learned that it's the ego that judges everything, right? As I sat in meditation over a several week period, asking for guidance and understanding about why music, and why now, I kept seeing and hearing signs that **this is not about me.**

So why so much resistance?

One of the other reasons I had not been singing beyond the confines of my private space, is because of the experience I had in 2005 that I mentioned in the beginning of this book. If you remember, it was while on vacation on the French Riviera that I had the blissful night of singing at a night club. It was not a spiritual song, it was *Fever* made famous by Peggy Lee, sung over a banging club beat to an audience of chic party people. The day after that bliss experience, I had the vision of my future in France where I was seen singing professionally.

What I haven't told you yet, is that on my way back to the US, I had one last stop in Barcelona. I once again stepped on stage to sing at an open mic jam session. That's where I met a beautiful singer/songwriter named Meritxell, the latin Queen of Soul. Her voice is truly mesmerizing and when we found out that we lived not 30 minutes away from me back in DC and we vowed to meet up when we returned.

Back in the US we connected, I sang live with her and her incredible band, and she even helped me out with a song I was writing about self-love, "I Love You, Me". Meritxell's music and live performances have always been awe inspiring, and to be honest, I felt like my talent was so small in comparison, that it wasn't worth putting a huge effort into pursuing. She was always supportive and encouraging, and I doubt she knows how much I admire her voice.

A mutual connection Meritxell and I shared was with a doctor named William Tedford, or Dr. T, as he was affectionately known. Dr. T always booked the most amazing musical talent for his National Professional Network cruises. Meritxell had performed on the cruises he organized in years past and one year I sang as well. On that cruise Dr. T admitted that he had no idea that singing was a passion of mine because, as usual, I only showed up as the Dr. Andrea everyone knew from the TV.

For the last two years that I lived in Washington, DC I sang at some of Dr. T's local events, he was a true supporter of mine.

And since my move to France and my transition to living as my Authentic Self, I did start to sing more. I kept in contact with Dr. T and told him about my desire to work on music more. He told me he would certainly have me singing at one of his future events. Tragically, that never happened.

In February of 2019, Dr. Tedford ended his life. And while the details are unfolding slowly and are not mine to share here, I can say that I was visited by his spirit. Well, it was through a friend of mine, Kitty Waters. While speaking with her via video conference, just days after Dr. T's death, I expressed to her my devastation that we lost another soul to depression and suicide.

I explained to Kitty that I felt an urge to do even more to help people who are suffering in silence. At just that moment, Kitty told me she could feel Dr. T's presence! I had no idea she had that ability, and I was shocked when she said that Dr. T was telling me that I must SING NOW. As tears fell down my cheeks I could sense his presence with us. It was then that I remembered one of the last conversations I had with him where he told me he would have me sing at one of his events.

That week, in honor of Dr. T, I decided to silence my inner comparison critic and sing live on Facebook. I was choked up with tears, but I sang *My Funny Valentine,* one of my favorite jazz songs, one that he appreciated, too.

My soul has longed to express emotion through my singing voice, and apparently other souls have wanted to hear it, too.

Honor your dreams, they are the treasures of your soul.

By acknowledging and accepting the need to fulfill our desires we embark on our journey to wholeness. I feel whole and fully integrated when I express my creativity, especially through music. I do not want to go back to the silenced, censored version of me, so in 2019, when I was scheduled to give my 3rd TEDx, I decided I would use the opportunity to sing.

I had already been booked for the event, but the life transition of Dr. T prompted me to take to the stage and bring forth the last element of me that I was hiding. So for my talk at TEDx Peterborough in April of 2019 I sang part of *I Love You, Me* live. While my inner critic would love to point out all of my vocal flaws, my soul is at peace. I feel that I have finally honored my soul's wish. The song I wrote so many years ago, has finally been revealed to the world! (Visit www.RealSelf.love to watch it.)

Sister Jenna contacted me the week that TEDx went live with yet another confirmation that the arts and singing are, in her view, a clear soul calling. While I've had multiple signs and calls pointing and pulling me toward signing over the last 15 years, I don't know if I could have fully embraced singing as part of my spiritual path before now. I consider the people who dial into their true spiritual destiny early in life the fortunate ones. But I do think that we all have a soul urge to follow a life path that brings us closer to full integration of all of our parts, and full expression of our Authentic Self. I have fully surrendered my ego, and now feel aligned with my destiny.

Which brings me back to the concept of self-transcendence. Remember that in life we begin with desires tied to basic human needs, as Maslow described with his hierarchy of human needs. We go from pursuing the basic biologic and physiological needs, such as safely, food, water, warmth, and sleep, to the safety needs, which include security, stability, and order. As we ascend the pyramid toward self-actualization we eventually arrive at a knowing, a deep awareness that there are goals even beyond self-actualization. Expressing my inner most feelings and thoughts on stages, podcasts and TV shows as my Authentic Self is me living fully self-actualized.

Singing for the sake of my soul and the connection to others, to the Divine and to music itself, is about transcending my lower self. I now recognize that the desire to sing and express myself musically isn't coming just from my personality or musical background. It's beyond all that.

So remember that the pursuit of self-transcendent goals including being of service to others, and being meaningfully connected to the whole world, God, or a higher calling is also worthy of pursuing. These kinds of goals do not have to be pursued for fame, money or recognition. That's proof that they are going beyond, truly transcending the lower self.

No matter where you are on this upward trajectory know and trust that your soul is behind, within, and above guiding you every step of the way! Recognize that while there may be times that you have desires for self-gratification, nurturing, and pleasure, these are not indications that you are trapped in selfish ego-land — unless you infringe on the rights or respect of others.

Behind the scenes your higher self is nudging and urging you to open yourself up to the possibility of living a life where you joyfully, wholeheartedly, unashamedly, and unapologetically express yourself. The Authentic Self motivates us to be true to who we really are and to share ourselves with the world in meaningful ways.

What secret dreams or fantasies about the type of life or contribution you'd like to make to the world have been with you for a long time? What would open up for you if you decided to surrender and say 'Yes' to expressing them?

In your journal or in the space provided at the end of this chapter, make a list of the secret desires, wishes, fantasies and longings you feel deep inside. Some of these may be basic needs that you must fulfill on your journey to self-actualization. And some may be the true calls of your soul. By writing them down, you honor them and give them the opportunity to be seen, acknowledged and quite possibly, to be expressed.

Values

Your driving force and motivation

The other aspect of you that is intrinsically *you* is your value system. What you value in life can be clearly reflected in your lifestyle, your relationships and your career. I say that it *can be* seen in those areas of life, but we all know that sometimes we tolerate situations and people that don't really match our ideals. But if you were really living in full integrity, aligning your life with your values, they would match.

Becoming aware of your personal values can reveal hints about higher aspects of your Authentic Self. When you recognize that your values guide your actions and decisions toward wonderful, significant contributions you can enjoy pleasure in life without guilt. You can use the awareness of what really drives you to make positive, life enhancing changes.

So what do you value? What drives you? What motivates you in life?

In my first book, *The Pennington Plan*, I outlined a 5-step motivational strategy for achieving your goals. Using this plan in my life and with clients for over fifteen years now I realize that defining your motivation, can be pivotal for many clients who have major goals that involve high stakes, or long trajectories for their accomplishment.

In that book I ask you to list five reasons why you want to reach your new goal. For example, if you want to get married and start a family you are prompted to give five motivating factors for achieving the goal. When we have more than the obvious reasons on our mind we go below the surface needs to contact the soul. The soul has desires and urges it wants you to fulfill in this lifetime. By exploring the 'why' you arrive at what the achievement would *bring* to you and what it would *mean* to you.

This meaning is what you place a high value on. In other words what you highly value is what can motivate you to put in the work to reach the finish line.

Our values provide an unseen energy force, a determination to push beyond perceived limits, laziness, procrastination, self-doubt, and other useless limitations.

I love the way that my friend and colleague, Jo Simpson, the author of *The Restless Executive*, talks about a values. She has developed a values discovery process which includes three steps: **discover, define, and ignite.** *Discovering* your own values means that you're going to look at all of the things in your life that have shown you what you really value, cherish and hold dear. Then *defining* what those values *mean* to you really helps you get clear on what you stand for and what you won't stand for. Simply defining your own values, lets you know why you've done certain things, why certain people fit in your life and why others do not.

When you can tell which parts of your life or relationships are not in alignment with your values, it's much easier for you to decide what to shift. The third part of Jo's values process is *ignite*, which means you put your values into conscious action in all your decisions, and activities; the way you speak, in your relationships and of course, in your goals.

As an example, I deeply value integrity. Based on dictionary definitions most people think of integrity as adherence to moral and ethical principles; soundness of moral character and honesty. To me integrity represents wholeness and congruence. I see it as being fully aligned in words, feelings and actions. When my beliefs, behaviors and speech are aligned, in sync, then I am living in integrity and I feel comfortably aligned.

When interacting with people who say one thing, but act in a way that goes against what they say, I feel the lack of congruence with all of my senses. It sounds as bad as someone singing off key. It smells like rotten cheese. It feels like having a knot in the pit of your stomach. My whole being becomes a sensor for alignment with that value.

Have you ever experienced something like that? Perhaps when someone confided in you about their negative feelings about someone or a situation, but the very next time you saw them they acted as though they liked or agreed with that person. When someone is not acting in ways that line up with their feelings, beliefs or ideals then it points to dishonesty on one level or another. And that drives me crazy!

I also highly value freedom. When this value is threatened or disregarded, I am deeply aware of it in my whole self, even if not through language. If I feel that I am being blocked in expressing myself or prevented from exercising my will in some way it creates a negative feeling of tension inside me. Because I place a high value on freedom and because I cannot tolerate my liberty being blocked I have set up my life, work and relationships to honor this value. In this way, my life is aligned with my highest values.

When we talk about alignment, congruence, or integrity — it means that things line up for you. Things match. Things are in harmony. Living in alignment with your values will allow you to create more harmony and joy because you'll be attracted to people and situations that fit you naturally. This applies in business as well. As my friend Deri Llewellyn-Davies says, going against company values, or breaching the values of an organization, is enough to get you fired.

In my life, if someone's values don't match up with my own or their behavior goes against what I value most, that's also grounds for them getting removed from my life. And this is important because when you have a clear idea of your values — and you have actually written them down or said them out loud — it makes it so much easier to create your boundaries and prioritize meaningful goals. Imagine if you lived with such conviction.

Are there principles that you live by? These are likely your intrinsic values, they define who you really are on one level.

Another way to discover your values is to look at it from the negative and answer this: What are the things that really tick you off? List the things which really irritate you or irk you; your pet peeves. If you list all the things that really annoy you, you can work backwards to define your values. For example, if you get really upset when people are late or cancel appointments with you at the last minute this may point to a high value on timeliness or courtesy to honor your commitments and respect for your time.

Your values are at the core of who you really are. They form the basis of what you hold most dear and how you judge whether or not, something or someone is important to you. When we're aware of our values and make a commitment to align our lives with them, we move away from the m'ego's selfish biases and preprogrammed reactions to become conscious co-creators of our lives.

Outside influences on values

Of course, our parents influence our values and our upbringing can shape them as well. So if you grew up in a family with an emotionally distant parent you may have come to really value closeness and togetherness because you missed out on this as a child. On the flip side, if you had a very smothering parent, an alcoholic parent or so many siblings that you never had time and space to yourself, you might really value freedom and alone time.

Whatever the objects, feelings or circumstances are that you truly cherish or that you would fight for, those are your values. And when you can align your life, your work, your relationships, and your play around your values, you will find it so much easier to live your life authentically.

It is important to note that what we value can often be something considered negative. In other words, values can have a negative edge to them. If for example you've grown up in a family that did not appreciate your outspoken, boisterous nature, you may have adopted a tendency to be quiet or to conform. This reactionary compensation may have caused you to value conformity. Rather than rocking the boat, you may actually prefer to be with people and in circumstances that don't allow for much divergence from norms and agreed upon standards.

The m'ego, driven by its fear of being hurt, shamed or destroyed, often generates characteristics that fuel our behaviors and interactions with people and circumstances. Through our lives some of these emotional drivers get activated and may even form habitual ways of operating in the world. They form the underlying paradigms that dictate our self-expression — but only up to a point.

Have a look at the qualities listed in the two tables below and circle any that apply to you. Are there any fear-based emotions that are driving how you live your life?

Fear-based emotions	
Competition	Victimhood
Scarcity	Criticizing
Self-interest	Blaming
Conformity	Resentment
Martyrdom	Envy
Closedmindedness	Revenge

The heart-inspired, love-based values provide a higher, evolved, and loving perspective, a lens through which we view ourselves and the world around us. Circle the values from the love-based emotions box that most resonate with you. It may help to think of times in life when you were inspired to take action for yourself or someone else. What moved you from within to take action? A simple example is offering directions to someone who looked lost — even though you were pressed for time. You may have been in touch with your value of compassion or the wish to be of service to another person in need.

Have you ever found money or something of great value and you went out of your way to get it to the lost and found or a responsible party who could ensure its safe return to the rightful owner? That's honesty and integrity at work.

Love-based values	
Collaboration	Creativity
Expansion	Abundance
Contributing to others	Love for family
Creator	Integrity
Uplifting	Honesty and Authenticity
Accountability	Trust
Forgiveness	Celebration
Compassion	Generosity
Inspiration & Hope	Respect

I value integrity, authenticity, freedom, and creativity. These are the things that drive me in all that I want to achieve and in all that I want to feel. So when I look at the areas of my life and the roles that I play, these values are my standards. They're my personal principles that dictate what I allow into my life and what I will *not* allow into my life.

So what about you? What are those deeply held beliefs, standards, or ideals you live by or would like to live by? Start to make your own list of values.

No matter what society is doing or what your parents or your BFF think, your values are your own and they really do link to your Authentic Self.

Summarize your personal values list

Because we use values as a measure of what drives us to move toward or away from someone or something, this is one list you really want to have written down. Before moving on, affirm for yourself, "What I value most is... What I enjoy in life is... What motivates me most in life is... What drives me in my life is..."

And then on the flip side ask, "What really irritates me? What frustrates me? What will I simply *not* tolerate?"

Are you driven by love, freedom, a sense of belonging? Or is it fun, adventure, exploration? Maybe it's contributing or helping others, or establishing deep connections. Perhaps learning and constant discovery are important, too. Do you value your health and vitality? What about honesty? Trust? Independence? Which of these words resonate for you? Write them down and add your own to make a list of your personal values.

Finally, return to the list of 21 Virtues mentioned on page 80. Are there any virtues that stand out as ones you admire or would like to embody more? Make a list of those as well.

Paradigms of Possibility & Your Personal Success Mantra

When you look over the list of your top strengths, values, and character traits can you see how they've helped you, guided you, and motivated you on your life journey so far?

To make it even more obvious, write down three or four accomplishments you've had in the last few years. List anything positive you achieved, from getting a new job or promotion, to successfully organizing a bake sale, to consistently preparing healthy meals for your family, to quitting smoking, or saving $500.

Now consider what made these achievements possible. Certain values, virtues, capabilities and talents mixed with determination and perseverance created a field of possibility. It's a good practice to explicitly list them.

Let's say that one accomplishment was baking an amazing new bread for a family event that everyone enjoyed. If someone asked, "How did you do that?" You may respond at first with the details such as, "I bought a cookbook and followed a recipe." But if you were replying to someone from another planet who knew nothing of the operating rules of planet Earth, how might you explain it more clearly? What underlying principles made it possible?

You might say something like this: "There's this thing called yeast which causes bread to rise. With the right ingredients, tools, and recipes I can make delicious bread for my family."

Now explain what about YOU enables this to happen? What factors in **you** made it possible? This could be your talents, values or passions.

Maybe one of these statements fits: "I love feeding my family tasty, healthy meals." Or, "I demonstrate my love through action."

You could summarize it this way: "I use my love for my family, my creativity, and my ability to follow directions to prepare delicious food. In short, I am creative and capable of amazing things, especially when doing them for the people I love."

For most people, the ingredients for personal success seem obvious to them, especially if they come naturally. But it's important to really see and feel the power of the assumptions or underlying beliefs at play that empower your actions, decisions, and outcomes. This opens you up to unseen potential for advancing your life on every level.

As you explain how you achieved each of your accomplishments, no matter how trivial, write down a single statement about the underlying belief or paradigm that allowed you to achieve that success. That single statement will serve as your own personal success mantra.

Here's another example:

What I achieved: I lost ten pounds and kept it off.

How I made it happen: I exercised five times per week and ate fewer sweets.

Why I did it: I value my health and my body.

My underlying paradigm: I am disciplined to be active to maintain my health and energy. I follow good eating principles to stay fit. I appreciate my healthy body.

Use this format to investigate several accomplishments and the underlying principles for your success.

Recent Accomplishment:

_____

How I made it happen:

_____

Why I did it, what motivated me to do it:

_____

My underlying paradigm:

_____

After you've written down how you achieved a few things over the last year, now do the same thing to explain how one or more of your peak experiences were possible. Write down which strengths or talents were engaged. List which values or desires provided the fuel to see you through to the completion of your goals.

Here's an example from one of my experiences I shared earlier:

Peak Experience: Singing at a club in St. Tropez

How I made it happen, which strengths were active: I combined my love of music with bravery.

Why I did it, what motivated me to do it: I used my desire for creative self-expression to sing from my heart.

My underlying paradigm: I am boldly following my heart and living my dreams to share from the heart and inspire others.

Peak Experience

_____

How I made it happen, which strengths were active:

_____

Why I did it, what motivated me to do it:

_____

My underlying paradigm:

_____

Since most of us are really good at focusing on the things that _don't_ go right, such as the failure to reach goals or the mistakes we make, it can also be helpful to examine our disappointments to turn them into fuel for more excellence.

It can be tempting to look at specific mistakes and pronounce judgment on your overall value or worth. But that's as silly as looking at a six-month-old baby and labeling her a loser because she falls down while learning to walk. We know that unless she has some major physical or neurological problem, the baby will pick herself up and one day she will not only walk, she will skip, jump, and run.

Based on your innate strengths and determination to be your best self, I invite you to consider that hidden in your spiritual DNA is the ability to rise up from challenges and move forward.

Instead of judging, let's proactively learn from our failures and mistakes and embrace our true nature — which is to fall, and then get back up!

Make a list of three or more disappointments from last year. Explain why each happened. Consider what really led to those disappointments. Where did you fall short? What excuses did you make for why you weren't successful?

Next, considering what you know today, what could you have done to make them be successes instead? What would you do differently if facing similar circumstances? Write your new paradigm of possibility as an affirmation that is consistent with the results you'd like to have.

Here's an example:

Disappointment: I didn't save as much money as I wanted.

Why it happened: I made too many impulsive purchases online. I didn't make regular deposits from my paycheck into my savings account.

My new paradigm: I am committed to saving for my future. I will consciously follow a budget and appreciate my growing savings account.

Past disappointment

_____

Why it happened

_____

What explanation or excuse did I use to justify it

_____

My new paradigm

_____

Write Your Personal Success Mantra

The explanations you wrote down for all of your accomplishments, peak experiences, and even your disappointments represent the **paradigms of possibility** for you. Now let's summarize them into powerful, positive, personal belief statements that will serve as your guiding principles for living an awakened life. When you're motivated to reach a goal or to make a move to overcome an obstacle, returning to these statements of possibility will remind you of your source of power, and provide you with the mental outlook necessary for achievement, which is in line with your highest sense of self.

Look at the reasons you wrote down which explain why you were able to achieve your accomplishments and what made your peak experience possible. Look at the explanations of why your disappointments happened and what you would do differently to avoid those disappointments.

Now summarize your capabilities and underlying philosophy into a single powerful, positive statement about who you are, this is your Personal Success Mantra. To write yours, remember to include the baseline assumptions that were in place to make each of your achievements happen. It's also a good idea to include the values or attitudes you possess along with any relevant character strengths and talents.

For example, to explain why and how I moved myself and my daughter to the French Riviera I reply:

"I am committed to a life of vitality, joy and peace. I am brave. I value freedom. I boldly follow my heart and I live my dreams with passion."

This positive possibility statement includes two of my values and character strengths, freedom and bravery, and it states in a positive way how I choose to live my life. This statement is what I return to any time I feel a hint of doubt or fear when embarking on a new project.

By repeating my Success Mantra from time to time during periods of stress or worry, I remind myself that as a courageous, freedom-loving person I can choose to trust my heart and live on my terms. This is especially useful since *this statement is based on evidence in my life where it held true.* It is based on real past experiences. It's not a flimsy affirmation of who I wish I could be. Even if I'm faced with a situation that is not exactly like the ones I used to get to my Personal Success Mantra, I know that the characteristics underneath the statement are real and true.

Your Success Mantra should be stated in the present tense and as a positive statement. In other words it should contain phrases like "I am…" instead of "I don't…" or "I can't…"

Bring your mantra to mind anytime you need to be reminded of your power, your focus and your belief in your abilities. Your Personal Success Mantra can lift your spirits dramatically the more you repeat it, read it, or see it. (They make great inspirational postcards for social media, too!) Over time you'll find that your Success Mantras won't need to be repeated very often; you'll simply live your life in accordance with your deepest truth. You could even write several Success Mantras, one for each area of your life that you're consciously working to improve or transform.

My Personal Success Mantras

_____

_____

_____

_____

_____

_____

_____

_____

_____

_____

_____

_____

Lastly, look back over the dreams, desires and longings you've felt. If you've been wishing to express yourself fully, pursue a new line of work or course of study, or if you've been dreaming of creating a business or or launching a charity, consider what belief system would make those possible for you now. Your Paradigms of Possibility should now provide the spiritual fuel to pursue the things that you truly value, the ideals your soul would ideally love to explore. Be bold and write down here some of the big dreams you'd love to explore in life. These will be investigated further when you start to architect your Diamond Life in Chapter 6.

My Deep Desires, Dreams & Wishes

PART II
TRANSFORM: LOVE WHO
YOU ARE

Love *You*

Have you ever heard yourself ask, "Is this all that life has to offer me?" Or have you ever said, "There's got to be more to life than striving, competing, hustling, and hurting"? We've all felt hopeless at some point in our life. Questions like this are a good sign that you're hungry to awaken to the truth of who you really are and what your life could really be like.

Now consider these questions...

What if you could take steps today to remember and *live as who you really are and who you were meant to be* — before the programming and socialization process took hold?

What if by living from your *strengths and talents* and authentic character traits your friends, family, and the world at large could see and appreciate the real you?

What if you began to love who you are right now, which then allowed you to shine a light of unconditional *self-acceptance* that set others free to do the same?

All of this, and more, is possible for you. No matter how bleak your life may look now, I can assure you that a better life of confidence, self-acceptance, and bold self-expression awaits. You are just one decision away from living your life as your most authentic, audacious, and awesome self.

Wait... could it really be that simple?

The Cornerstone Process
Step 2 — Acceptance

Can I accept ALL of who I am, just as I am?

In Step 1 we recognized that since the physical realm is only one aspect of your existence it is NOT the definitive factor determining your self-worth or self-expression. Now, in this second phase of transformation you will learn how to allow "what is" to be as it is, without resistance or judgment. You learn to accept the vessel you were born into, not as a limiting factor in your life, but as an ally. When you come to accept the present circumstance as it is and realize that the past is behind you, you'll feel the power you have now, in this present moment, to consciously architect your future.

Similarly, when you can accept that your parents and society followed a common path of socialization and treated you in ways determined by their own limited understanding of life, you can come to accept and forgive yourself and others as who you and they really are. You'll learn how to stop making judgments of right and wrong about your past, your parents, or how you are put together, and ease into acceptance of what is present in the here and now. Rather than fighting your natural impulses because you fear what others will say or think about you, you'll learn to accept your desires as they are.

Now before you start accusing me of encouraging you to become a doormat, please know that **acceptance does not equal passivity, complacency, or tolerance of negative treatment**. It's simply a point of non-resistance to what exists in the here and now. By accepting who you are and the processes that led you here, you'll gain the power to move beyond them. If you continue to resist, deny, or otherwise avoid looking at and accepting who you are, you run the risk of perpetuating the situations and beliefs that block the power of authenticity, creativity and love in your life. This will only keep you sick, alone, unhappy, and broke.

Don't worry, in this book you'll learn several techniques to decrease resistance, stress, and fear while releasing the negative beliefs and emotions locked into your body, mind, and brain. And if you've got deeply resistant beliefs holding you back, I'll show you how you can join us for a live event to clear those blocks and put you on track for a liberated life.

Likewise, I'm not advising you to settle for impulses that are selfish just because they feel like they are at the foundation of the real you. You may recognize that you feel an intense drive to succeed, achieve or build up wealth to finally feel safe based on your early life experiences of lack or despair. Once you see this urge for what it is, you can go beyond it to a more peaceful, positive drive.

As you learn to accept who you are, another key concept will become clear, which is, you must release all of your self-judgments about what you think you "should" be based on the expectations of others. To accept who we are in this present moment requires that we let go of the often unrealistic ideals of what could or should be, but just isn't. During this step we explore the many hidden beliefs that may be locking you into a state of personal rejection and even self-hatred. And you'll be happy to find that forgiving yourself as well as others of their shortcomings or judgmental attitudes becomes easier.

For my own journey, self-acceptance was a long and arduous process because I had several parts of my personality that I call 'Supreme Court Justices' to contend with. It was as if I had several judges in my head scrutinizing my every action, thought, and desire. Like a courtroom drama, they sat in judgment to determine which of my goals were worthy of pursuit, which accomplishments merited recognition, and they constantly assessed how very far away from perfection I almost ALWAYS was. The bar was set so high by this internal court that it was simply impossible to please them, which is why I often felt like a hopeless failure.

By working through my awareness activities, Step 1 of The Cornerstone Process, I discovered how these internal judges became part of my personality as a result of my upbringing and early childhood experiences. As I gradually questioned their validity, I came to realize that not only were they fictitious, a silly illusion created by my immature subconscious mind, I discovered that their attitudes, assumptions, and judgments were wrong! They didn't line up with my true personality, my spirit, or my ideals. I was then able to accept who I really am — the me I always longed to be — and I found the courage to let the real Me have some room to breathe, move, and even play! I learned to kick those internal judges and their judgments out of my head. In doing so, I moved on to Step 2 of The Cornerstone Process Acceptance.

3

Become Mindfully Aware of Your Human Tendencies

"If you are pained by external things, it is not they that disturb you, but your own judgement of them. And it is in your power to wipe out that judgement now."

~ Marcus Aurelius, Meditations

It's quite possible that despite the wonderful qualities and talents we've uncovered so far you still doubt how amazing and glorious you are. That may be due to repeated experiences in your life that made you question your worth, doubt your lovability, or think that you're broken, defective, or stupid. Or you may come from a culture or family that taught you to avoid calling attention to yourself or to not show off or brag, and those influences might linger today. It could be that during your death in a past life you locked in beliefs that you deserve punishment, or that you are worthless. Perhaps, based on past mistakes, you consider yourself flawed and with that conclusion you've given up on the possibility of being accepted and loved.

In many ways, we are trained from birth to aim for unrealistic, often unattainable goals for our appearance, behavior, and attitudes. From our childhood upbringing, to the media influences, religious messages, and our peers, we are programmed to compare and compete with others for acceptance and approval. Sadly, we often lose our inherent flair for originality and mold ourselves to be like the crowd, to fit in and get along. When we're not mindful of this background programming, we may automatically react to social situations in a self-judgmental way. The impact this has on our self-image severely hampers our ability to truly enjoy life.

Despite your past, no matter your mistakes or shortcomings, you are an amazing human being, capable of greatness, and worthy of love, happiness and achievement.

Any judgments about your worth or lovability that were made based on the m'ego personality, or when you were at an immature stage of development, or made during a past life were not made about the REAL present you. Therefore they are *not* valid. Any point in your life where you weren't living as your Authentic Self is not subject to critique or ridicule. *Now* is the time for you to accept yourself completely so you can live with peace and joy in your heart as your Authentic Self.

For some people learning that the real you was forced into hiding or molded into submission by the influences of others makes them feel sad or mad. You may find that guilt, anger, resentment, and frustration surface when you realize how these past influences and programming have caused you to veer off course from living your true passions and dreams. I certainly did, at least for a while. Eventually I realized how pointless it was to fight my nature — no matter the amount of peer pressure. It was futile; I could no less turn a dog into a platypus. I am what I am. I also realized it was useless to hate or blame my childhood experiences or my parents, for they were set up to recreate what they were taught, too.

Maybe it's also time for you to stop changing to meet anyone else's standards. The good news is that the parts of you that were wounded or sent running for shelter within can be reintegrated via a gentle recovery process.

There is no reason to wallow in self-pity. No time for victimhood here! Feeling bad about the way you were conditioned to react to life isn't going to take you far anyway. Rather than bemoaning our fate or crying over lost time we can instead, use our energy wisely to bring peace to the present and optimism for our future. It begins with **Acceptance**, Step 2 in The Cornerstone Process.

Accept what is, release what was, declare what will be.
You have the power!

It is much more empowering to acknowledge that the past brought you to this very point, and now you're conscious of those influences. Rejoice in your awakening and recognize that **every dysfunction served a function** in the past. Now you are free to make new choices.

Reframing our negative tendencies into positive traits

It may sound like a cliché, but all the problems of our personality truly can be seen as useful in some contexts. Are you willing to consider alternative understandings of problematic aspects of yourself? How many ways can a "negative" aspect of self be viewed as useful? In what context could the problematic factor be considered beneficial? Viewing supposed negative aspects of ourselves or our lives as having a silver lining may serve to increase self-acceptance. The difference between an ordeal and an adventure may be in the way you look at it.

While participating in a sacred retreat in Iceland, I went on a mystical journey led by two shamans that made this point crystal clear for me. Aided by sacred songs, drumming and plant-based medicines, I experienced a visual and emotional exploration of several life issues. First I was shown how every person, circumstance, goal and activity was laden with judgments, assessments and labels. I literally saw and felt the weight of these judgements, and though this was a mental movie playing in my mind, it was totally exhausting. I was, at first, overcome with shame and disgust that, despite my spiritual path, I was still filled with so much judgment.

In this vision I saw how I reflexively labeled, judged, and assessed everything in my life. For a while I sat there in total self-judgment for having these tendencies. I wanted to puke it made me so sick! Then, I would wipe away the images in my mind when they became unbearable. As the ceremony continued another scene would appear to be investigated. And once again, I was shown how much judgement and labelling I had going on. I was filled with a sense of condemnation. So I'd blast the image away again, it was too painful and too draining to see and feel.

After a while of looking at scene after scene, I finally recognized that I was totally resisting the lesson that these visions were meant to show me. So instead of pushing the images away in disgust, I allowed them to be present. As soon as I relaxed and surrendered, I was magically transported to a subdomain, a world in my psyche underneath the surface of judgment-laden circumstances.

As if looking at the basement of my subconscious mind, I saw an aspect of my personality, let's call her the 'Judgmental B**tch'. And it was clear that she had a really good handle on how to make my surface life work. Though I experienced the heaviness of all of the good vs. bad, right vs. wrong labels, from her deeper perspective, it was clear that her drive for excellence was helping me in my day to day life. Based on her underlying system of selecting things that are in line with my values and ideals, my everyday life was actually pretty orderly. But on the surface, I mistakenly judged it as harsh perfectionism.

Of course, attending a shamanic journey put me into a deep state of introspection and the entire experience opened up portals of consciousness that allow for deeper understanding, but I wonder if you can get a glimpse into some of your behavior as well. I was able to journey through multiple layers of my consciousness and sense the energy of my life choices. On the surface level everything is quite dense. But when we dive deep into the subconscious we see life in symbols, metaphors and patterns.

This ceremony revealed to me that my tendency toward judging my own perfectionism was leading me to shame and pain. When I understood that this trait, as mentioned earlier in this book, is a part of my true nature, it became clear that it is not meant to be purged from my life.

Now matter how a negative trait lodged itself in my psyche, when I can find and embrace a positive aspect to it, I can then manage its expression for my benefit. Getting rid of a trait like perfectionism may seem a worthwhile goal given the negative consequences it produced for me in the past. But I eventually realized that it would be draining and a waste of my time because it's ingrained in and part of my nature.

Can you see any traits that you have or society has labeled as wrong, bad or undesirable that may actually be serving you in a constructive way?

On the positive side, many clients have told me that they value how thorough my presentations are, and the excellence with which I conduct business and create holistic programs — which is all due to my perfectionistic streak. I have since reframed this trait as an aspiration toward excellence. This is also one of the character strengths identified in the Values in Action survey you took in Part 1 of the book. This trait shows up on a spectrum: those who don't express much of the trait may seem apathetic, while others are controlling and perfectionistic.

Over time I have become more at home with myself, less self-deprecating, and more at ease with living in a way that doesn't feel like a constant battle between the deepest part of me, and what may be expected of me. When I sense that I'm allowing myself to tend toward perfectionism, I remember the negative repercussions and adjust the dial on this trait.

What is the opposite of self-acceptance and how does it manifest?

Self-loathing, self-hatred, self-denial, and self-suppression are the opposite of healthy self-acceptance. The results of remaining in these self-deflating states include: low self-esteem, depression, denying yourself pleasure, not engaging in certain activities, hiding your body, fear of freely expressing yourself, fear of rejection, not living authentically, being fake or trying to mold yourself into some imaginary ideal, and not speaking your truth.

The bottom line is that when we do not accept ourselves fully and unconditionally, it's hard to believe that anyone else would accept us unconditionally and we feel constantly threatened by potential rejection. We may hide our true feelings or suppress our emotions, which leads to a constant sense of threat that these strong feelings could erupt and overtake us at any moment.

Remaining in these threat-based emotions and with threat-focused thoughts, narrows our choices of how to respond to life. When we face critical, threatening, or judgmental interactions — whether real or imagined, from another person or ourselves — our brain perceives them as an attack. Studies show that living with this self-induced stress causes the brain to remain in a vigilant mode of protect and defend. Our brain prompts us to fight, flee, freeze or even to adapt our behavior to appease others. Never feeling good enough compelled me to strive for achievement at the cost of my well-being.

It's in our best interest to root out the fears or hidden emotions that leave us feeling threatened and find ways to create a feeling of safety to keep our entire brain physiology open to pleasure, free self-expression, and confidence.

The Gentle Path to Self-acceptance

Your next step is to take your newfound self-awareness and rejoice in the fact that you can embrace a new possibility for living as your Authentic Self. Your past experiences brought you here but, the past need not limit or define you. You can instantly access incredible power, strength, and courage to craft a new self-description that corresponds to the empowering image originally outlined by your spiritual DNA. You can recreate your life according to the true image of you.

Soon you'll rewrite your life story as an inspiring, heroic tale of victory and self-realization. But first, in this chapter we must uncover and deactivate any hidden landmines in your psyche, to truly set you free. With an open field of creation cleared of negatively charged psyche-bombs we are invited to construct a living temple on a foundation of enduring self-love.

So how *can* you embrace and develop unconditional self-acceptance? There are three keys we'll explore in this chapter: **living mindfully, practicing self-compassion, and embracing your own unique essence**; what makes you authentically special. These keys, when fully utilized, will unlock the door to your entering into and boldly living your own epic life.

If we are not mindful and aware of the emotions that are driving our behaviors we will blindly go through life like a robot.

It is, of course, next to impossible to be compassionate toward the feelings that we repress and refuse to acknowledge. If we get carried away by our negative emotions we can become melodramatic and wishy-washy. So learning to balance **mindful awareness, self-compassion,** and **authentic living** will help us overcome our tendency to feel self-conscious and self-critical.

Harvard psychology professor and social scientist, Ellen Langer, Ph.D, the author of *Mindfulness and Self-Acceptance* says that one of the simplest and most natural methods of reducing self-evaluation and replacing it with acceptance is to assume a mindset of mindfulness rather than mindlessness. So we'll start there.

Mindfulness

Most of us go through our lives totally oblivious to the source of our internal attitudes, mindlessly assuming that our mental dialogue and belief systems are accurate. I've never heard someone openly say that they thought they were unlovable. But with this hidden belief in the back of our minds we are driven to act unnaturally or to strive for accomplishments to minimize the chance of being discovered for the imperfect, unworthy being we assume ourselves to be.

Most of us are unaware of how much shame of falling short of some unrealistic ideal controls us. It is our mindless assumptions, which inhibit us, bind us, and rob of us self-expression. Left unchecked, these mindless assumptions influence nearly everything we do in life, especially in our relationships.

Mindless Assumptions—The "Shoulds"

Are you aware of any "shoulds" floating around in your head, such as, "I should be further along in my career by now." Or "I should already be married with children." How about "I should be living on my own." These typical "should" statements are the types of thoughts my clients tell me rattle around in their minds all day long. Becoming aware of what's taking up your mental energy is an important part of mindfulness.

Mindfulness involves a more flexible mental state where we draw new distinctions about the present situation and the current environment. When we are mindful, we are actively engaged in the present and sensitive to both context and perspective. From what perspective are you evaluating yourself? In the context of your current lifestyle and demands on your time, is it realistic to judge your life against some arbitrary ideal?

Rather than remain in a mindless state of constant self-evaluation and self-criticism, mindfulness encompasses an attitude of self-acceptance as we are called to shift the focus of our attention to acceptance and exploration of *present* experience. Consider what is new and different about this time in your life that you can accept and appreciate.

Where did this "should" come from?

As you've learned, the way we express our inborn temperament depends on our experiences and environment. The experiences of day-to-day life cause us to react in ways to protect our identity if we perceive them as threats. As impressionable children we simply reacted without thinking of the long-term consequences of our choices. We responded automatically based on primitive instincts of self-preservation. The lasting effects of those habitual coping strategies make us feel uncomfortable because they're not moving us forward to what we desire in our lives *now*; living authentically with confidence.

The various defense mechanisms and self-preserving actions we adopted may have served us when we were young children, but the underlying assumptions, beliefs, and biases may no longer hold true when seen in the context of our present environment and desires for the future. From where we stand today it's our self-image or m'ego that guides our actions based on what it believes is realistic or safe to accomplish. But if you're twenty-five now, you wouldn't want a five year old determining what you can or cannot do. The level of consciousness that a kindergartner possesses is simply too limiting.

The bottom line is that some of your conditioning created habits or patterns that may be holding you back from really loving your life, creating exciting goals, and embracing opportunities for growth and expression. It may help you to understand, that you're not alone in all of this! Few of us have grown up with a perfect sense of self. It's part of what it means to be human.

Whether spoken audibly or internally, we are often driven by urges that are not in line with our personal truth. We've been programmed to do things out of obligation, for fear of being rejected, and out of a need to please others.

If you could drop the "shoulds" and accept that here and now you're open to live life on your own terms; how would that make you feel? Could you adopt a more playful perspective and look for ways that you can express your Authentic Self?

For the next 21 days notice every time you use the words "should", "must" or "ought." Notice when you think "I should call Jane back." Or "I should, must or ought to <u>fill in the blank</u>". **Ask yourself, gently, "Is it true?"**

Most of my clients they find themselves weighed down with the self-imposed obligations that are not aligned with their true desires. And if you look at the root of the word 'shoulder' you find that it is 'should.' So no wonder we feel such a heavy burden on us!

If you find that the internal voices of loud, obnoxious or really convincing "shoulds" exist, you will find the deep psychological techniques of transforming your internal dialog in Chapter 4 helpful.

Be Mindful of Your Human Tendencies

Mindfulness comes before compassion. In order to be kinder to yourself, it's helpful to realize that as a human, you have certain tendencies that are inborn. Rather than resisting them, if we accept that they are part of the package we inherit as a human animal, then we can learn to live with more tolerance and compassion — both for ourselves and for others. This will lead to a greater level of self-acceptance and self-love.

Below is a list of several characteristics inherent in the human experience to help you make sense of how you can bring more peace and power to your life.

We seek approval and acceptance.

We humans are like pack animals who want to be liked and accepted. Our ancestors' survival depended on it. One million years ago, humans needed to be accepted because trying to live without a tribe meant you lacked protection and possibly food. Since it's a natural human tendency to seek affiliation or belonging, we are naturally predisposed to seek approval. This means that our primitive brain will also cause us to do anything to avoid rejection or disapproval.

When we're driven to avoid criticism or rejection it's hard to do anything in life authentically, wholeheartedly, or passionately. Instead we go along with social norms and give up some of our inherent brilliance and purpose. And we judge ourselves based on those social norms. Unfortunately, we seldom realize how mindless and useless it is to base our self-worth or self-acceptance on the need to be better or at least, "as good as" other people. No matter how much we polish or puff ourselves up, there will always be other people who are more attractive, more talented, or more *whatever* than we are.

Think about your own life. In what ways have you adapted or changed your behavior in order to seek approval or acceptance? Chances are those adaptations are deeply engrained now. And they may be based on your natural talents and tendencies, just taken to an extreme. As you move toward acting solely on conscious choice now, consider how those traits could be flipped into assets.

We are self-conscious.

It is a natural human tendency to become self-conscious. The most important question is: what do you consider to be the *self*? In the wise words of Tara Brach, psychologist, Vipassana meditation teacher, and author of *Radical Acceptance* and *Living with Your Heart Wide Open*, "if your identity is limited by or linked to the ego, you will always live with self-doubt." A sense of vulnerability and separation will always be there. Because the false self's attempt to feel better by getting approval and attention doesn't really address who we really are, we feel an endless hunger for affirmation.

So how do you identify yourself? Do you still categorize yourself based on the roles you play? If I asked you to describe yourself, would you respond with something like, "I'm a mother." Or, "I'm a teacher." Or do you identify with your personal status or accumulations, such as, "I'm a six-figure coach"?

Sadly, most people tend to classify their own self-image into rigid categories. They often see themselves, not as individuals with innate self-worth, but as a thrifty person, a beautiful person, a slowpoke, or an emotional person. This type of self-categorization based on accomplishments, jobs, possessions, or age is too narrow and limiting. What happens to your self-worth when that category no longer applies to you? If you get divorced, lose your job, or your wealth, will you no longer accept yourself? Will that make you less valuable? If you categorize yourself within the narrow boundaries of "wife," "millionaire," or "CEO" you could be left without an identity if and when those things go away.

Likewise, if you identify yourself based on a perceived "flaw" or limitation, you'll experience life in a severely limited way. No inspiration there, right? For this reason I'm also against labeling yourself with a disease, such as saying, "I am a diabetic." This too, puts limitations on you personally, and can color the way others perceive you.

We have many facets of self. We must discover a larger, more authentic sense of who we are beyond the ego-based self. We can lose the inherent beauty of our own existence if we narrowly categorize ourself. Instead, when we choose to view ourself mindfully, openly, and with flexibility — rather than rigidly in narrow roles — our self-image becomes rich and full of possibilities. We can then recognize our own right to enjoy love and the pursuit of what makes us happy at each stage of life.

How could you define yourself now that leaves room for the possibility of joy, fulfillment, and pleasure in life?

We have a near constant internal dialogue or self-talk running through our minds.

It's a natural human tendency to have some sort of self-talk or mental commentary going on in our heads throughout the day and night. Becoming more mindful and aware of how we talk to ourselves is a worthwhile step to becoming more confident in our everyday life. Since we humans are predisposed to a narrative in our head about our looks and abilities, we should make sure that it's a positive and accurate one.

By mentally reminding ourselves of our uniqueness, our gifts, and our talents we can replace the negative self-talk that steals our joy. Each day, remind yourself of three elements of your personality, appearance, or ability that are beautiful, funny, or special. Say it out loud to yourself while looking in the mirror.

One of my clients, Leslie van Oostenbrugge, The Awakening Dentist, says that to pull herself out of a negative tail spin, she would regularly affirm that she was smart, good looking and awesome while looking in the mirror. She says you should not be shy about expressing and celebrating what makes you unique and special. This is not about bragging, it's about self-acknowledgement. The Buddhist Monk, Ajahn Brahm, author of *Don't Worry, Be Grumpy,* says that "You don't get big headed when you practice self-compassion and praise yourself. You get big hearted."

Thupten Jinpa, the English translator of His Holiness the Dalai Lama, and author of *A Fearless Heart*, also encourages us to examine our self-talk and our self-critical thoughts. He suggests that we deliberately look for ways to turn those negative statements into more compassionate ones. (More on his compassion training in Chapter 4.)

We have a hater within: Our inner dialogue often sounds like a bully.

I have clients who tell me is that there are haters out there, so-called people who judge or criticize what they're doing. The presence of these haters causes them to quit working on their new business idea, or they get out of a relationship, or they stop engaging in a hobby. All because they say that the criticism from other people bothers them and makes them feel self-conscious. The intense feelings of being judged and criticized leads them to doubt their own decisions.

Others have told me that they don't start projects because they already know that a colleague, or a friend, a family member or some other "hater" is going to throw shade or criticize them. Some people are so paralyzed with worry that they won't embark on a new journey or life path, out of near certainty that others will comment, criticize, or ridicule them. They fail to start or they abandon projects too soon, all because they're so worried about what others will think.

Sound familiar?

Now I realize that given the prevalence of social media in our daily lives it's quite possible that there are people out there who might be hating on you. The reality is, however, that *we* are normally the ones imagining all sorts of negativity being thrown our way that just isn't real.

Quite often, the hater is you. Almost all the negativity is in your head. By that I mean, the people you imagine would or could say negative things about you have been allowed into your mind **by you**. In fact, the internal sound of their voice is so loud, you really believe that it's real. But the truth is, the voice in your head belongs to you. And even if the words sound like something a hater would say, you can choose to listen or not. And even better, you can choose to stop the negative self-talk and release your inner cheerleader.

While you may be tempted to dismiss this as some sort of fluffy affirmation junk, take heed of your inner dialogue, for it is what feeds your brain. The negative voice in your head acts like a nasty little gremlin that dumps doubt on you and sucks away your confidence. If you put up with negative mental chatter, and accusatory or snarky comments, your brain is going to remain in the watchful stress-mode. We must learn to identify, challenge, and disprove these negative thoughts and replace the voice in our head with positive, supportive, and compassionate thoughts.

Here are five ways to overcome the negativity of your own inner conversation to bring you more peace and set you on the road to greater success and happiness. I've included several techniques from clinical psychology in the next section for the deeper, darker voices, and inner wounded child. But to start with, these simple steps will put your body, brain, and mind into a more empowered state.

I. Become aware of the mental script in the background of your life.

Which phrases do you hear most often rumbling through your mind?

Do you engage in any self name calling. For instance calling yourself a dummy or an idiot?

How about the tone of the voice in your head? Is the voice nasty and mean?

II. Question and challenge the voices.

Ask yourself, "Is it true?" And be honest with yourself!

III. Disprove the inner commentary and expose the lies by finding evidence to the contrary.

For example, if you hear an inner voice saying, "I always mess up!" Look for evidence in your life where you didn't mess up.

IV. Replace the lies with truth.

Seeing that those comments are not totally true, replace them with statements that are true. Remind yourself that you are competent, smart, helpful, and worthy of success. Look at the Personal Success Mantras you wrote down in Chapter 2.

V. Take positive action to affirm your power.

Go out and prove your case. Use your talents and abilities in a way that is meaningful and positive that shows your inner meanie that you are powerful, positive and capable. Taking action is the best way to set the new intentions and new language into your mind and heart so that they last.

The mirror deceives us.

I have suggested that you consider that there is more to "you" than what you see reflected in a mirror, what is printed on your resume, or what you've accomplished in life. Has that sunk in yet? Are you the same "you" that you saw in the mirror ten years ago? Are you fundamentally the same naive teenager from high school?

Beyond self-acceptance, I believe that developing a foundation of genuine self-love is essential to healthy relationships and authentic living. True self-love is based on knowing your Authentic Self, beyond body and behavior. At the core of your being, is a perfect, divine essence worthy of all the love and devotion in the world. This is something that the mirror doesn't show you.

Have you ever been with someone and found that you could look past their physical body as you connected with them on a deeper level? Have you found yourself loving someone or feeling deeply drawn to someone, based on a light that shines from *inside* of them or an energy that they radiate *out* to the world? This goes beyond the physical, and it's evidence that you are not your body or behavior.

Beyond the visible changes in our appearance, at a deep level we are always evolving. Therefore, it's healthiest to think of yourself as a "work in progress." Studies in Ellen Langer's laboratory showed that when participants replaced fixed words such as "is" and "am" in their self descriptions with possibility words such as "may be" and "could be," they enjoyed increased productivity and creativity. Which rigid words in your self-narrative can you substitute with possibility words?

As humans, we all make mistakes, we'll all age, we'll all experience sickness, and we'll all eventually die. Accepting your own humanity will allow you to release the unrealistic expectation of always having a youthful physical appearance or achieving a socially promoted "ideal." And recognizing these hidden tendencies within you will allow you to offer more compassion to yourself and others. Remember that you are not alone when you feel the uneasiness associated with the passage of time. So give yourself a break and let go of striving to maintain a fixed image of yourself.

Take a moment to reflect on the beauty and wisdom of your current stage and age in life. Can you appreciate how you have more to offer this world now?

We are critical or ashamed of our bodies.

Besides our self-judgment about our behaviors and desires, the critical self-evaluation of our bodies can also derail our pursuit of our dreams. While most of us are painfully aware of the ways we criticize our body shape or appearance, we're not always conscious of *why* we judge our bodies to be anything less than perfect, in the first place. We are often clueless about the social, cultural, and media influences unconsciously providing us with a gauge as to whether we measure up or not.

When I moved to Atlanta, Georgia to attend university, I became really mindful of some of the cultural influences that impact body shape preference. While living in "Hotlanta" I was hit with a barrage of comments from some black men about my body type. I have a naturally slim build and I quickly discovered that for many men of color, their feminine ideal is that of a woman with a large, curvy booty. In fact, I would regularly hear men refer to me as too skinny! Before relocating to Georgia I wasn't self-conscious about my body shape. Instead, I have always recognized and accepted that I have features from both my mother and my father that make me unique. I never thought of myself as lacking anything. Perhaps growing up in Colorado where there were fewer curvy booty women around gave me a sense of normalcy.

My experience with professional modeling in my teens and twenties also helped in this regard. It sounds crazy that I came out of my modeling days with a healthy sense of self-acceptance when we hear of extreme stories of women who go to great lengths to be bone skinny in the fashion industry. For me, however, as a model and an actor I came to understand that the casting directors often had an idea in their head for the character they wanted for the campaign or stage production. If I didn't fit the mold, I assumed I simply didn't have the overall look they wanted. I didn't take it personally and I didn't feel rejected. It never occurred to me that I wasn't beautiful or talented. It just didn't cross my mind in that way.

In university I began to study the effects the American culture and media have on body image and self-acceptance. I could see very clearly that the promoted social ideal was arbitrary, it varied with time and geography. It wasn't fixed. My friend, Marie Fiorin, jewelry designer, fashion blogger, and author of *How to Be Delicious*, encourages women to realize that the "ideal" body image changes every decade, and has, for the past hundred years. If were to you look at magazine covers from the last few decades, you'd see that there's been a different body size, shape, and look that the fashion industry and media deemed ideal.

In the fifties the hourglass figure was the ideal, so the pencil skirt, belts to accentuate the waist, and a prominent bust were featured widely in advertising. In the seventies we saw a more androgynous body type as the feminist movement arrived on the scene. At that time women rejected constraining bras and burned them. At this point the less buxom woman was celebrated. In the eighties and nineties the arrival of supermodels like Claudia Schiffer saw boobs come back on trend. And currently we are in the era of the big booty, wherein derriere lifting jeans and surgically implanted butt enhancements are on the rise. Women with big butts can finally rejoice. The popularity of Jennifer Lopez, Beyoncé and other women blessed with large posteriors should help us understand that there is something lovable about each of us... and there are lovers out there who will adore and cherish our bodies just as they are.

According to the Renfrew Center Foundation for Eating Disorders, during the last fifteen years only 5% of women naturally have the body type portrayed as ideal in advertisements. Trends come and go season after season. Plastic surgery to change your appearance every five years would be physically and psychologically detrimental. And you never know if your new face or body shape will be in, or stay in, fashion when you're done. So, as Marie says, make the best with what you have.

In what ways have you felt inferior based on your body type? Are you mindlessly judging and comparing yourself to an imaginary ideal? What would happen if you decided to love and appreciate your physical body for the glorious gift that it is?

We long to be cherished.

Wayne Dyer, once said, "You are privileged to have the body you have. Honor it as if it is the garage in which you park your soul. Refuse to have contemptuous thoughts about your soul's garage, your body. Don't complain about its size, color, or worn-out places... Treat your body like a guest who visits and then must leave. While it is here don't neglect it, don't poison it. Honor it, welcome it, and allow it to take its course which is ultimately to leave as it came, back to where it came from. Make it fun to watch your body go through its designated phases. Be in awe of every inch of it."

As you cherish that precious body of yours, why not adorn it with beautiful clothing, scarves, perfumes, or oils in celebration of your inherent beauty and sensuality? Just as you would pamper a new sports car, nurture your body with tender loving care. Just as you might drive that new car around town to turn heads, allow your body to be seen and appreciated. This is not about exhibitionism and there's no need to go overboard with designer clothes or expensive accessories, but tasteful attention to your wardrobe and appearance can enhance the pleasure you enjoy in your life. Expressing your love and appreciation for the body that temporarily houses your spiritual essence will allow you to experience life with more appreciation and joy.

Have you heard comments from a lover, your best friend or a trusted family member praising your appearance, personality, or other personal attribute? How often do you dismiss those compliments? Remember that we are all attracted to different qualities for many reasons, sometimes odd ones, too!

Be mindful of the compliments you receive and rather than dismissing them, appreciate that in the eyes of that person, they behold your beauty.
Cherish yourself just as you want others to cherish you.

We hide our flaws.

When there are parts of ourselves that have been devalued or that people have made us think are unacceptable, we often avoid expressing them in order to avoid rejection. For example, some of my clients are afraid to express their anger or rage.

They consider these emotions to be wrong, bad, immoral, or unspiritual. Thus, the part of their personalities that feels anger is stuffed away, silenced or otherwise de-energized.

Others may have hidden their sensual or sexual side because they associate sex and intimacy with immorality. Whether it is because they have been programmed by religion to believe that premarital sex is a sin or due to a past experience of sexual abuse, some people determine that sex is bad and shameful and the part of them that is entitled to a fulfilling sex life is shunned and blocked.

Based on those programs, what happens when situations arise in which they feel angry? What do they do when sexual urges occur? The person who assumes anger or sensual pleasure is undesirable may consider themselves to be negative or wrong for having those emotions arise in them. The conflict between what they feel (anger or sexual desire) and what it says about them (they're bad, evil, defective, non-spiritual) creates an uncomfortable emotional condition — and in some cases physical pain.

Besides emotions like anger and natural life urges like sexual desire, some people have taken on the beliefs that getting attention, nurturing or even rest are signs of weakness, laziness or self-indulgence. Does any of this resonate with you?

These inner conflicts can even cause a person to shut down and withdraw from life. A removal from life, whether externally seen or inwardly practiced, leads to an inauthentic life. This suppression of emotion means the energy behind the feeling cannot be expressed, released or transmuted. However, this energy will not disappear entirely. Either it remains stocked up, bubbling within, only to erupt at some point in the future, or it slowly eats away at the human body and mind causing physical illness or mental stress.

Anger explodes into rage, violence, or abuse. Sexual desire seeks relief through promiscuous sexual activity, excessive masturbation, or relationship hopping. The need for attention, nurturing or soothing can lead to binging on food, shopping sprees or tearful outbursts and burnout.

Most often, the part of the personality that has these emotions gets pushed into the "shadow."

What is the shadow?

Carl Jung said that "the shadow is the person that we'd rather not be." He explains that the shadow is the side of our personality that we do not consciously display in public. It may have positive or negative qualities. If it remains unconscious, the shadow is often projected onto other individuals or groups.

Anything that we judge in others is often a hidden part of our self that we deny or of which we are ashamed.

Most of us think of our shadow as the hidden, nightmare version of our self, but it may also be composed of denied parts of our personality — including the qualities that might be considered positive — such as the successful, rich, happy, loving, and outgoing version of the self.

The shadow can be considered a normal, natural part of our personality and if we embrace it, nurture it, and give it a place in our lives we can grow, evolve, and become more peaceful and whole.

In the book *Romancing the Shadow,* Connie Zwieg, PhD., and Steve Wolf, PhD. explain:

"Beneath the social mask we wear every day, we have a hidden shadow side: an impulsive, wounded, sad, or isolated part that we generally try to ignore. The Shadow can be a source of emotional richness and vitality, and acknowledging it can be a pathway to healing and an authentic life. We meet our dark side, accept it for what it is, and we learn to use its powerful energies in productive ways. The Shadow knows why good people sometimes do 'bad' things."

How to discover your shadow

Debbie Ford, author of *The Shadow Effect,* encourages us to focus on what we love most about ourselves — like our generosity, openness, loving nature — then ask, "what would be the negative opposite of these qualities?" You'd then discover your shadow in you.

Since you don't like those qualities you tend to express the opposite. So, if you look at your currently expressed personality traits, you may find that your shadow is what encouraged you to embody them.

Just know that when you totally disown those shadow qualities you tend to become unbalanced and eventually those parts of your personality will express themselves in often explosive ways.

What we deny within ourselves we project onto others

In *The Shadow Effect* film with Debbie Ford, Deepak Chopra, and Marianne Williamson, they highlight several examples of people whose shadow has reared its head in aggressive ways. One such example is Mel Gibson who produced films about Christianity and in a drunken rage screamed anti-Semitic comments.

Katya Walter explains that the "Shadow wants to be heard, simply that. But if it isn't, it turns nasty. It becomes a veritable demon, witch, or son of a bitch, demanding its pound of flesh… in very painful real time, not dream time…. Pay attention to your shadow. If you keep distancing yourself, saying, "Heavens, it's not my fault!" — then heaven help you. Hell won't."

Shine light on your shadow

The gift of embracing these qualities and allowing them to be expressed in healthy ways, is that we become more open, free, and peaceful. We become more whole and balanced. By giving that part of our personality space to be, without total rejection and judgment, we become more accepting and tolerant of others who also express those traits. We then allow light to shine on those hidden parts of our personalities, and allow them to be considered "right" and acceptable, instead of constantly labeled as wrong or negative.

By embracing and accepting that we ALL have the potential for light, dark, diabolical, and angelic qualities, we recognize that we can embrace and accept ourselves as whole and complete. You may feel less tension in your life and more energy to live your truth when you're no longer using energy to hide your undesirable traits. You don't go on rampages, nor do you give in to the lazy, greedy, or other "negative" qualities.

Instead, you allow your feelings to inform you of what you really need... sometimes it's important to be "greedy" for personal time rather than being so generous you don't know how to say no or set boundaries. Sometimes it's important to let your "lazy" self teach you how to take a break, rest, and renew yourself. You then appreciate your active side.

At the start of this chapter I told you about **the three keys to self-acceptance: mindfulness, self-compassion, and authentic living**. To recap, **non-judgment, present moment-focus, acceptance and curiosity are the hallmarks of mindfulness**. You're now aware of how you've been programmed and/or wounded.

As you recognize that we all have some sort of neurotic inner dialogue or fear keeping us up at night, you don't have to give in to it. Stop comparing yourself with anyone else. Give up on comparing yourself against a societal or imaginary ideal. You can't ever become anyone other than who you are, so stop assessing your value, looks, or body against anyone else's. Affirm your right to gracefully be YOU. Instead of assessing how you measure up compared to others, affirm the positive, real attributes about yourself that bring you and others joy and pleasure in the here and now. Each day, remind yourself of three elements of your personality, appearance, or ability that are beautiful, funny, or special. Say it out loud to yourself while looking in the mirror.

For these beliefs to sink in and replace old programs there is some daily compassion work and a forgiveness meditation to help you in the next chapter. I recommend that compassion and forgiveness become a way of life for you. The stuff that happened to you in the past — whether it was your fault or someone else's — needs to be put into a helpful context. When you can recognize that everyone was just acting on their level of awareness and some of their actions may have been motivated by pain or anger or ignorance; little by little, you can forgive others and forgive yourself. And that's what's going to give you the power in the present moment to be free from guilt, pain, shame, anger and resentment.

To assist you in fully accepting just how worthy you are, just as you are, I have recorded two special interviews. Visit www.RealSelf.love to watch interviews with Monika Laschkolnig who shares a powerful poem for you. And the interview with Marisa Peer, the famous hypnotherapist and self-love advocate, includes a guided hypnosis audio track with simple phrases you can repeat to reprogram your mind to recognize and accept that you are inherently worthy.

To further assist you in reprogramming your mind, I invite you to take on the challenge of becoming mindful of your tendency toward negativity. For the next ten days, you'll be abstaining from negativity in the 10-day Negativity Fast.

The 10-Day Negativity Fast

This activity is kind of like a mental diet. For the next ten days, I want you to be aware of your mental chatter and internal dialogue. When you catch yourself thinking a negative or self-critical, derogatory thought, write it down. Challenge, flip, and dispute the thought. Then, replace it with a positive, compassionate one. By the end of ten days, you'll have a clear picture of the types of phrases you need to debunk and replace with a formal dialogue between your inner critic and a more compassionate part of yourself.

Some of my clients enjoy setting up a punishment for breaking the negativity fast. What could you do to ensure that you won't let yourself get away with being self-critical or negative?

Keep notes about your progress in your journal.

In the next chapter, you'll learn compassionate mind training, several healing practices, mindfulness exercises, and meditations that will get to the core of any past injuries and remove the pain along with any limiting beliefs that have been keeping you stuck. They're meant to empower you to live with compassion and become attuned to Truth in the present, so you can embrace who you are and live authentically.

For now, I would encourage you to celebrate the milestone of reaching the halfway point of this book. You've likely examined and challenged some of the thoughts, behaviors, and judgments that made up your identity. This is no small feat.

You may find that you're a bit raw or even emotionally numb. So, to keep a positive vibe coursing through you as you prepare to move into the deeper healing work ahead, consider the following exercise. Make it your daily practice from this point forward, if you haven't already.

The 3 Blessings Ritual

Each evening write down three things for which you feel blessed, grateful or happy. These could be things that went right in your day, people whose presence you truly appreciate or things about yourself of which you are proud. Expressing gratitude each day, in writing, creates new brain networks that will help you recognize and value the positive aspects of life, however small they may be.

While it is a natural human tendency to neurotically focus on negative things in life, we have the beautiful capacity to build up positive brain networks and joyful energy just by focusing our attention on the good that happens every day.

Don't neglect this deceptively simple ritual that can lead to joyful serenity day after day.

4

Heal Your Wounds & Reclaim Your Perfection

Some of my dear friends from Iceland friends explained the Icelandic translation of the word perfect. In Icelandic, the word for perfect is fullkomin, which literally translates to fully present, or fully arrived. The Icelandic concept of perfection then, is to be fully present — not partially present — but totally present, rich or poor, flat booty or big booty, zits, freckles and all.

Within the meaning of the Icelandic term fullkomin there is no hint that perfection relies only on the presence of favorable qualities while hiding the supposed bad ones. When you are fully present you can show up authentically, in all your splendor, just as you are. There is an expectation, therefore, that you are perfectly poised to interact with, connect with and benefit from whatever is present before you and within you.

I encourage you to proclaim that now is your time to heal your past, forgive yourself and others, and accept that you are a perfect soul living in a sensual body. Accept that as human beings we will always occupy bodies of different shapes, sizes and colors that will appeal to some but not others. Our bodies will change and morph over time; they'll get wrinkled and saggy. We'll never have utterly flawless skin. At least not all of the time. And we will make mistakes, hurt others, and even hurt ourselves. If we let go of the unrealistic goal of becoming a smooth skinned, perfectly proportioned, never erring robot and embrace our humanity, we can learn to celebrate and even savor our uniqueness.

We are perfectly imperfect.

Know That You Are Worthy Of Love Just As You Are

As a human being you are automatically worthy of love and affection, just as you are. The body that carries your essence, spirit, or soul through this life is not *you*. And since the body isn't really you, it should not be considered a limitation to your self-expression and self-enjoyment. There is no other being on this planet who is walking around with your precious and unique essence. In fact, the space you occupy in this jigsaw puzzle of life is uniquely designed to fit you and nobody else! There are other puzzle pieces out there, the souls in bodies who are meant to interact with and bond with you, that can only fit with and correspond to the authentic version of you. They are looking for the real you, so stop trying to be something you're not. You are lovable just as you are!

Remember that you are desirable for more than your looks, talents, and accomplishments. Even as your body or health wanes the energy or essence of you, your soul, is what people will be attracted to. Psychologist and Vipassana meditation teacher, Tara Brach, says, "The source of our well-being is an underlying sense of beingness, our basic nature of goodness." The more we relate to ourselves as precious beings with a basic nature of goodness, the more we will realize that we deserve love for no other reason than our presence on earth. Embracing a mindful perspective will also enable you to appreciate that the qualities other people have do not diminish your inherent worth as an individual. There's no need for competition or feeling less desirable than others. Focusing attention on the present moment and approaching the present with an accepting, open, and nonjudgmental attitude may also reduce your inherent tendency to worry about the future consequences of fading beauty or diminishing physical prowess.

To return to the wholeness, the basic goodness of who you really are, it may take some deeper healing work. This chapter includes several of the healing techniques I and my psychologist friends use in clinical practice. I taught many of these practices to clients who had endured significant trauma in their lives, including sexual trauma, because they are so effective at removing the pain, shame, guilt, and anger that can easily get locked into the body and brain when we endure painful experiences.

Please note that some of these practices, such as the Inner Child Dialogue, may be best practiced with a therapist, bodyworker, or coach who is skillful and trained in providing a safe space for processing raw emotion.

The more we relate to ourselves as precious beings with a basic nature of goodness, the more we will realize that we deserve love for no other reason than our presence on earth.

Compassionate Mind Training

Many of my clients who have lived for a long time with repressed emotions such as anger, fear, or shame find it hard to openly, calmly be with their feelings. So much so that even when situations in life show up with love, compassion, and kindness, they still struggle to let their guard down to receive praise, support, attention, or companionship. It's for this reason that I began offering compassion-focused therapy in my clinical practice. Professor Paul Gilbert, author of A *Compassionate Mind*, is a British psychologist who specializes in helping people overcome self-criticism and shame. He created a technique called Compassionate Mind Training, which enables us to deliberately cultivate mindful attention, acceptance, and our own emotion-soothing capacities. These techniques are proven to have a major impact on our brain function, which is critically important when we want to create new habits and a meaningful connection with our others.

Humans evolved to be social creatures and when we are connected emotionally and physically to others we thrive. Our brains have evolved to include pathways and wiring, which support attachment seeking, emotion regulation, and bonding. The old brain's survival focused fight, flight, freeze or appease response system often gets priority activation since it's been in our genes for millennia. Having such a sensitive threat-assessment system causes us to consider almost anything to pose a threat to our survival, including our own self-judgment. Dr. Gilbert's research, along with many others, shows that by tapping into compassion and self-soothing practices we can turn off our negative self-critical brain and focus on building emotional resilience. This all leads to more authentic living and more harmonious relationships.

The Practice Of Self-Compassion

The gentle energy of compassion can help the destructive energy of negative emotions to be transformed and released. Compassion is defined as being touched by the suffering of others accompanied by a heartfelt wish to alleviate that suffering. It also includes extending kindness and understanding to others even in the face of their "bad" behaviors or shortcomings. Underlying compassion is the recognition that we are all connected by our humanity, all subject to mistakes and missteps, and all worthy of kindness. Compassion is not about pity or about feeling sorry for someone. It is based on an understanding that the pain we see in another could happen to any of us. At its best, compassion reduces our tendency to blame or criticize others.

Over the years I've heard people say they were afraid that being too compassionate with themselves would lead them to become too soft or lazy. This rarely happens though. Self-compassion is not self-pity, self-absorption, nor self-indulgence. As Thupten Jinpa says in *Fearless Heart,* if we do not nurture our own compassionate heart, we will never be as fully alive as we can be or as present with others as we desire to be. We need to *"train our compassion muscle"* on ourselves so we can be even more attentive to the needs of others. The benefit starts with us and extends to everyone we touch.

Could you offer kindness and compassion to a friend who is dealing with low self-esteem, a personal setback or a perceived flaw? The answer is most likely yes. Now, in the face of your own mistakes or shortcomings are you extremely self-critical? With high standards for excellence and the unconscious pressure to be seen as superhuman, the mere idea of offering oneself the compassionate, tender and nonjudgmental treatment we would offer another seems foreign and even wrong to many people. So, the parts of us that are imperfect or less than ideal, get splintered off, stuffed into the darkness and hidden. This is how the shadow-self is formed. When we reject or hide parts of ourselves, we are left feeling fractured, disjointed and cut off from our true self. All too often we hide our true feelings and suffer in silence. Does any of this sound familiar to you?

Researchers in emotional intelligence, self-esteem, and self-compassion have written about the benefits of seeing oneself as inherently worthy of love and kindness. Moving away from the critical evaluation of the self, self-compassion moves us into a positive emotional stance where we extend feelings of kindness and caring toward ourselves.

Being self-compassionate means that whether you win or lose, whether you meet your sky-high expectations or you fall short, you still extend the same kindness and sympathy to yourself that you would extend to a good friend.

In the words of Albert Ellis, founder of Rational Emotive Behavior Therapy (REBT), self-compassion provides the individual with "unconditional self-acceptance," in which the self's worth is not rated or evaluated but is *assumed* as an *intrinsic aspect of existence*. This empathetic and compassionate experience will allow the previously judged and disowned parts of ourselves to be responded to and accepted in a caring way. Such self-forgiveness allows us to tolerate vulnerability and remain present and connected to others even in the face of our shame and human frailty. This empowers us to show up fully in our relationships and love wholeheartedly.

In contrast, when we cannot live with an attitude of tolerance and self-forgiveness, all that is left is to put up with self-criticism or live with shame. This can prevent us from showing up in life as our Authentic Self and connecting with others in the most wholehearted way because shame is a sense of unworthiness about our very being, not just about our actions. Shame comes from the words "to cover, to veil, to hide." And that is literally what my clients tell me they want to do when they feel exposed, vulnerable or "found out."

Judith Jordan, Assistant Professor of Psychology at Harvard Medical School and author of *Relational-Cultural Therapy*, explains that "the experience of shame is global and immobilizing. It often leads to withdrawal and isolation accompanied by a sense of self-blame and an inability to move back into the very connections that could provide repair." I know all too well how isolation prevented me from embracing healing relationships in the past. This is why today I am so passionate about getting this information out to the world.

Becoming mindful and tolerant of our painful emotions is the first step toward healing them and increasing our willingness to be vulnerable. As the beautiful work of shame and vulnerability researcher, Brené Brown, author of *Daring Greatly* and *Rising Strong*, so clearly points out, it takes courage to be present with others in the face of our self-doubt. Yet it's through the very act of being with others and sharing our mutual vulnerability that we can erase and undo the binding beliefs that we are not as good as others, or that we need to compare ourselves with others in the first place.

In the context of shame, we must first come to believe that we deserve respect and we matter in order to enhance self-acceptance and self-expression. This can be achieved through the practice of self-compassion as well as becoming more assertive and resilient. A supportive, compassionate attitude toward ourselves may also be associated with a host of other positive mental health benefits including less depression, less anxiety, less neurotic perfectionism, and greater life satisfaction.

So, what does it look like to practice self-compassion? What do we actually do? Here are a few exercises to light the path for you.

Wrap yourself up with a self-hug.

In times of intense pain or shame, do you find that a big hug is what you crave? My daughter taught me how she provides self-nurturing hugs when she feels that she's done something wrong or when she's sad or scared. She rolls herself into a tight little ball, like the fetal position, and will sit on the bed, in a corner, or on the bathroom floor with the lights off. This self-hug is her own self-soothing tool that seems to work wonders.

Why does a hug make us feel better? Research shows that by being snuggled up in the fetal position and through the act of wrapping our arms around ourselves (or someone else), we can trigger the release of oxytocin, the neurochemical that calms, relaxes, and makes us feel safe. While hugging and holding yourself, take deep slow breaths to help your brain recognize that you're physically safe. This triggers the relaxation response and gets you out of the stressful flight or fight mode.

You may find the same comforting feeling comes from taking a hot bubble bath, where you caress and soothe yourself in a womb-like watery cocoon.

Mentally retreat to a safe space.

The Safe Place meditation, described below, can be done anytime, anywhere. It involves visualizing a place where you could let down your guard and relax. You also imagine the feelings associated with being in a safe place. With repeated practice and regular deep breathing, you'll train your brain to get out of the stressful threat and defend mode on command. Over time, you'll teach yourself how to create calm and be at peace with whatever you want to examine or experience in your life. In this context you set up a safe place that you can mentally visit as you process any critical emotions or thoughts, or just to calm down. You can listen to or download the Safe Place/Relaxation Space guided meditation on www.RealSelf.love or do the practice as outlined below.

The Safe Place / Relaxation Space Meditation

In this meditation you will safely connect to a place of protection, comfort, and healing. Think of it as a mental retreat to a place of renewal where you can allow your body and mind to calm down. You will imagine a place of pure love and compassion.

It's helpful to find a photograph or painting of a place that you can easily imagine to be your own personal sanctuary for healing and relaxation. Would you feel most comfortable on a private beach? Perhaps a mountain cabin far from traffic noise or passersby would suit you. You may also choose to be in a mythical place, like in the clouds or on another planet. Wherever you imagine yourself to be safe, secure, and able to become relaxed and calm, bring this image to mind.

Begin by taking five deep, slow breaths to turn on your relaxation response. Breathe deeply enough to really fill your lungs to full capacity, then slowly release the air through your mouth, letting all of the air out gently and completely. It helps to make a sound as you exhale to fully release any tension or anxiety with your breath.

Next imagine that you are comfortably sitting or lying down in your safe place. Are you in bed? On a comfy sofa? Wrapped in a blanket or sitting by a warm fire? Let your mind build a scene that is inviting, cozy, and warm, where you feel cared for and safe.

I often retreat to a tropical bungalow all by myself. I imagine that I take a steaming hot bath and then wrap up in a soft robe and blanket to relax on a plush sofa. In my visualization, sometimes I'm alone, and other times I imagine that there are attendants who take care of food, maintain the temperature of the space, and keep me safe. From this place of calm, I can unwind, evaluate the stressful issues of my life, or just invite healing energy into my body and mind.

Decide what works best for you. Do this practice a few times to find out.

This safe space/relaxation place can also be a special location that you visit mentally to connect with a compassionate caregiver, a wise advisor, or healer. Whatever works for you, make notes of it in your journal. You may even choose to save a photo of the location clipped from a travel magazine for your journal or as a screensaver or desktop photo on your computer.

Once you're feeling calm, try the next intervention, which involves speaking kind, compassionate words to yourself while still in your safe place/relaxation space.

Speak Kind, Comforting Words to Yourself in Soft, Loving Tones

Each of us has an inner critic that can be quite hostile and say mean and negative things. This inner meanie can sling constant attacks at the part of us some call our "inner-target." For example, statements like, "You're such an idiot. You're hopeless!" We call this type of internal dialogue bullying. Our inner-target usually surrenders to these attacks, increasing our feelings of distress and helplessness.

In the same way that we have an inner-critic who can attack our inner-target in a cold and judgmental way, we also have a compassionate aspect of ourselves, an "inner-soother" that can comfort and soothe our inner-target by saying accepting things in a warm and compassionate way. For example, our inner soother might say, "It's okay to feel upset. You're not a bad person just because you feel bad."

Researchers believe that when you speak to yourself in a more compassionate way you activate parts of the brain associated with calmness and well-being, and deactivate parts of the brain associated with anxiety, stress, and depression. This is a skill you can develop and studies show by creating more compassionate self-talk you can also protect yourself from depression. Our goal, of course, is to empower you with self-soothing tools that will allow you to love and accept yourself more fully and unconditionally so you can be completely present and expressive in life and relationships.

To increase feelings of compassion and care, psychologists commonly recommend speaking to yourself gently, as if you were speaking to a wounded or frightened child, who we call our inner-target. I was familiar with how helpful this can be for my patients who had been abused or abandoned in their early years, but I had no idea it would be so beneficial to me personally. So, don't dismiss this one! (More on that later in this chapter.)

No one has grown up without having some sort of wound or disappointment from childhood that the adults in their life failed to fully address. No matter how grown-up we've become, how many degrees we have, or how big our investment portfolio is, there's still a younger, tenderhearted version of us deep inside. Your inner child may still need to hear the comforting, reassuring words of a caring adult, in this case — you.

Imagine a young version of yourself sitting beside you. Would you ever say to this innocent child that she needs to look a certain way in order to be loved and accepted? In the same way, you can quietly affirm your inner child's desire for unconditional acceptance.

In *A Fearless Heart*, Thupten Jinpa says that you might instinctively feel protective toward this child, thereby offering tender loving care rather than negative judgment or criticism. He suggests that while thinking of this image of yourself as a child, "let these feelings of tenderness and caring toward your child-self permeate your heart." Make an effort to connect with a spirit of gentleness, kindness and compassion, and feel the warm energy of compassion well up inside of you.

Mettā: The Compassion or Loving-Kindness Meditation

The Buddhist Mettā meditation, also called loving-kindness meditation, is a popular compassion-generating practice of directing well-wishes toward oneself and to others. For thousands of years, entire cultures have used this practice to remain kind and loving in the face of adversity and abuse. Mettā is a Pāli word that involves the desire that all living beings be well. It is more than just a feeling, it is an attitude of friendliness. From a Buddhist psychology perspective, if loving-kindness is directed toward our own suffering then self-compassion can arise, while if it is directed toward the suffering of others then compassion for them can develop. Co-founder of the Insight Meditation Society, Sharon Salzberg, the author of *The Power of Meditation*, describes loving-kindness as an unconditional love without desire for people or things to be a certain way, and an ability to accept all parts of ourselves, others, and life.

Below is a simplified version of Mettā Meditation, the loving-kindness meditation as written in *The Issue at Hand* by Gil Fronsdal of the Insight Meditation Society.

To practice the loving-kindness meditation, sit in a comfortable and relaxed manner. Take two or three deep breaths with long, slow, and complete exhalations. Let go of any concerns or preoccupations. For a few minutes, feel or imagine the breath moving through the center of your chest — in the area of your heart. Mettā is first practiced toward oneself, since we often have difficulty loving others without first loving ourselves. Sitting quietly, mentally repeat, slowly and steadily, the following or similar phrases:

"May I be happy.

May I be well.

May I be safe.

May I be peaceful and at ease."

While you say these phrases, allow yourself to sink into the intentions they express. Loving-kindness meditation consists primarily of connecting to the intention of wishing ourselves or others happiness. As an aid to the meditation, you might hold an image of yourself in your mind's eye. This helps reinforce the intentions expressed in the phrases. (You can receive a free daily audio inspiration as part of our 21-day Compassion Meditation Challenge. Visit www.RealSelf.love for details.)

I can tell you from personal experience that the Mettā meditation practice is profound. Besides the inner transformation that comes from finally being kind toward myself, I've recognized a clear shift in the relationships in my life. And clinical research is finding the same results in a variety of different settings. In fact, the loving-kindness meditation is growing in popularity among psychologists and therapists.

In 2016 a study published in the journal of Clinical Psychology and Psychotherapy found that just three weeks of loving-kindness and compassion meditations increased acceptance of the present-moment experience in people with borderline personality disorder. There were significant improvements in the severity of borderline symptoms, self-criticism, mindfulness, acceptance, and self-kindness. Likewise, a 2014 study in Spain found that for self-critical individuals, the loving-kindness meditation was effective in reducing self-criticism and depressive symptoms, and in improving self-compassion and positive emotions. These changes were maintained three months after the intervention.

The benefits of reciting or thinking the simple phrases of the loving-kindness meditation improve love and social connections, too. A study in 2010 by Drs. Cohn and Fredrickson showed that participating in a seven-week loving-kindness meditation course helped to expand love and improved health on a personal level for participants. Follow-up one year later showed that course participants experienced an increase in positive emotions over time, which led to an increase in resilience resources, including mindfulness, self-acceptance, social support, and positive relations with others. These resources, in turn, predicted life satisfaction and reductions in depressive symptoms. Similarly, a 2015 literature review of studies on the effect of loving-kindness-based interventions showed that practitioners experienced an increase in self-compassion and compassion for others and increased positive feelings and feelings of connectedness toward strangers.

To soothe and comfort ourselves, compassion researcher, Kristin Neff, author of *Self-Compassion: Stop Beating Yourself Up and Leave Insecurity Behind,* believes in the power of guided meditations and affirmations. She has also modified the loving-kindness meditation into a few short lines. With your hand on your heart Kristin invites you to repeat the following phrases silently: "May I be safe. May I be peaceful. May I be kind to myself. May I accept myself as I am." Her research confirms the wonderful benefit self-compassion can have on our overall well-being and even confidence.

I have recorded a guided meditation practice which includes the Mettā meditation. You can listen to and download it by visiting the Resources section of www.RealSelf.love.

Self-Soothing To Process Painful Emotions: The Two-Chair Technique

Sometimes it can feel like we are so far from lovable that practicing compassion is met with intense resistance. If you find that you are being extremely self-critical or relate to yourself as a loser, an unworthy person, or otherwise "bad," you may find that the two-chair technique, another type of self-soothing work is useful. Conceptually, self-soothing work is the antidote to self-criticism. It works not by suppressing the self-critical process but by integrating the unresolved emotional pain that *underlies* the self-criticism.

We are not born hating ourselves nor is it natural to harshly judge our bodies or behaviors. Remember, *you are not intrinsically self-critical*. Rather, you learned this behavior to adapt to the environment in which you grew up. As children, we are naturally in a state of pure self-acceptance. We don't know any other way to be. However, when we encounter a person of authority or high standing who makes us feel that we are somehow bad, wrong, or unacceptable, we may learn to challenge and criticize ourselves just as they did. Consider how bad a child could feel about themselves by growing up with an abusive or critical father, an emotionally distant mother, or after being bullied at school. People who have endured early experiences like this can become highly sensitive to threats of rejection or criticism from the outside world, and can quickly become self-attacking. Unfortunately, they experience both their external and internal worlds as easily turning hostile. Unless the child learns to soothe herself or has another parent to help her put the abuse into a less painful context, it is possible to carry the initial pain of rejection or criticism with her throughout her life. The reason for the long-term effect lies in the developing brain.

Dr. Paul Gilbert says that normally the ability to self-sooth develops in a context of secure attachment with early caregivers. However, if during our formative years we experienced abuse or neglect, the brain's emotion regulation system, which is responsible for self-soothing and safeness, does not develop properly because we must invest most of our attention to detect and respond to threats. In this context, a self-critical style may become internalized as a safety mechanism to prevent further abuse. This is particularly true for those of us who have felt a strong need to "be in control" of our emotions, out of fear that we will be rejected or perceived as being weak for having strong emotional reactions. Thus, there is a split within our personality: one part is self-judging and critical and the other feels unworthy, shameful, and guilty. As a result, some of us may end up forcing the unacceptable parts of ourselves into the shadow, suppressing our true feelings or denying our own needs.

The part of us that feels judged or criticized, our inner-target or wounded inner child, often develops her own voice and an overarching sense of powerlessness and vulnerability. Our inner child may speak in terms like, "I'm always screwing things up. I can't believe how weak and emotional I am." Because this part of us feels like she's under attack or at least under extreme scrutiny, the primitive, protective part of the brain gets activated. As you already know, if the threat-assessing part of our brain is active, we'll not likely feel confident to express our true desires in life. This type of inner dialogue will often prompt us to behave in ways to minimize further rejection — even if we are the ones rejecting ourselves! We may withdraw in shame, or sabotage a relationship or project; there are many ways the inner child can avoid potential rejection.

In similar fashion, there can be a part of us that has internalized the judging schoolteacher or critical caregiver leading our inner critic to carry on a mean, bullying type of rant such as, "You are so worthless! You really think people will listen to you? You're pathetic and you can't even control yourself to not eat a whole bag of cookies!" The inner critic's self-attacking voice can also push us to crumble under the intense self-scrutiny or withdraw completely in shame. This type of mental setup makes it pretty hard to feel confident enough to try new things, put ourselves out there in life, ask for a raise, or move to a new place.

For several years I ran an Intensive Outpatient Program (IOP) for women with binge eating disorder in my wellness center, which included the use of acupuncture and compassion-based therapy, among other practices. The years I spent with the brave women in the program taught me about the power of the inner critic's voice and the healing potential of bringing the dialogue out to be examined. Nearly every one of the clients had a strict inner critic that judged their overall worth, their bodies, and their every move, specifically their eating behaviors. When we tried to teach them about their eating disorder and its origin, the inner critic often tried to fight the healing process. The clients' binge eating was the only "soothing" behavior that reliably calmed down the intense neurochemical storm by triggering a tiny rush of dopamine.

Handling the conflicting emotions of fear, vulnerability, and powerlessness and the real desire to be free of the disordered eating behavior was a complex and challenging task. Over time many of my clients could see how their inner critic was trying to protect them, albeit with unhealthy consequences. Therefore, from the standpoint of the inner critic, giving up the coping strategy (self-criticism and binge eating) would be seen as foolish and the judged self easily gave in and began bingeing again to regain a sense of control, thus restarting the whole process over and over.

As I saw with my clients, engaging in a self-soothing dialogue can be helpful when we are truly ready to heal and become whole, loving, self-accepting people. Self-soothing work is meant to acknowledge the old underlying pain while helping you to access and build internal resources to support your healing and growth in the present. The deeper purpose of self-soothing, is to help you experience validation of your pain and transform your sense of being unworthy and unlovable to being worthy and lovable.

A basic assumption guiding the compassion-based interventions described in this section is that in order to resolve the split between our critical self and the harshly judged self, a dialogue should be enacted and experienced. It's not enough to intellectually understand the split process. It's necessary to actually experience the emotions of each part of the self to undergo emotional transformation and integration. Acting it out verbally and physically with a therapist, coach or in a group therapy circle can be helpful.

Psychologists, like Dr. Gilbert, often help clients get in touch with and process negative emotions left over from childhood with the two-chair technique, a gestalt therapy tool. Gestalt therapy is type of psychotherapy that focuses on gaining an awareness of emotions and behaviors in the present rather than in the past. The two-chair dialogue, which I have also used extensively with my clients, has assisted people in challenging their self-critical beliefs and helped them transform negative evaluations of their desires and needs into self-acceptance.

In this self-soothing intervention, you are asked to engage in conversation with a different version of yourself who is sitting in the chair next to or across from you. This could be your inner critic or your wounded inner child. As re-experiencing the pain could be overwhelming, you may choose to do this with a therapist to better handle and avoid being flooded by emotion. If you do feel capable of facing the fear and pain alone, the following exercise may be just what you need to really confront the sources of your judgmental and critical thoughts and to move beyond them.

There are two key processes involved in the integration. One is transforming critical feelings of anger or disgust into compassion and empathy, and the other is transforming shame into resilience and assertiveness. The inner critic is allowed to unleash her feelings of contempt and the part of us that feels judged is allowed to express her feelings of shame and powerlessness. The judged self can eventually tap into and express her own feelings of anger, which then helps her to better resist self-critical attacks and behave according to her authentic needs. Through an open dialogue, even the critical self can see how her emotional attacks are not helpful and she may adopt a more compassionate stance. These two processes can ultimately lead to negotiation and integration between the parts of the self and to new possible responses in the present.

You have the choice of starting with the dialogue between your inner critic and your wounded, judged self, or to start by allowing your judged self to open up to her feelings in a dialogue with your present, compassionate self. I'll begin by describing how to dialogue with your inner critic since this is often the strongest and most dominant voice.

Inner Critic Dialogue

Get two chairs and sit them across from each other. One chair will be for your inner critic while the other is for your judged self. Based on the research of Dr. Leslie Greenberg, we call the two chairs the "experiencing chair" for the inner critic and the "other chair" for the judged self, or inner-target. You will sit in each chair in alternation to express the thoughts and feelings of the two parts of you.

To begin, think about a time in the past when you were critical of yourself. Or imagine the type of situation where you are normally critical of yourself. What does that inner critic say? Are there common phrases that come up? Is she a bully trying to make you feel bad with her words? While sitting in the "experiencing chair," you will find that this part tends to begin with her normal reactions such as complaining or whining before moving to an inner exploration of current wishes or desires. Once you have a clear understanding of that voice, move on to find the voice of your judged-self by switching to the "other chair".

Think about the part of you that feels harshly judged, attacked or hurt by the critical voice. You're looking for a voice that disagrees with the inner critic or feels victimized by it. What does the judged voice say? The judged self in the "other chair" tends to use a lecturing self-judgmental type of voice initially, full of "shoulds" and negative self-descriptions.

Once you have a clear understanding of the different voices, close your eyes and imagine the past situation that you came up with previously. Allow the inner critic voice to speak. This can be inside your head but it's more effective to speak this out loud while sitting in the "experiencing chair". Allow your inner critic to speak for a minute or two.

Now, move to the other chair and repeat the process with the judged self's voice.

Allow a dialogue between the two voices to continue by switching chairs. Permit each voice to fully get out the emotions, feelings, and thoughts. Ideally each part will be able to hear and notice the feelings of the other. Usually, the dialogue will continue until a softening occurs in the level of emotion. The judgmental inner critic's voice and content will usually soften, become more understanding and even compassionate. It should become clear when you've gone as far as you can.

Give yourself time to calm down while taking five deep breaths. You may choose to speak compassionate tones to yourself from the standpoint of your present, adult self. Or use the voice of an outside person, your compassionate image as described in the section below, for example.

Write down what you observed. Are you more aware of the past influences that led you to become self-critical? Can you see why that judgmental part of you developed? Was it trying to protect you? Are you willing to give up the criticism now? What would need to happen for you to let go of this harsh judge? Write down these observations in your journal.

Inner Child Dialogue

Another way to use the self-soothing process is to enact a dialogue between the wounded inner child, described as a younger, tender side of the judged self and your present, compassionate adult-self. The first step in working with the wounded inner child involves connecting to the emotional pain, a sense of despair or anguish from the past. When we look at the pain with compassion and bring acceptance for the pain we discover that there is an existential need for those painful emotions to be processed. Processing emotional pain involves acknowledging the pain and allowing the pain to be seen and heard without censoring or judgment. Then we begin comforting the wounded self, and offer new, alternative insights to heal and move beyond the hurtful past.

To start a dialogue with your wounded inner child begin by imagining or physically creating a peaceful, safe environment where you will not be interrupted for at least an hour. This can be done with two chairs in your physical space or it can be done in your imagination.

Invite the wounded, scared, or shame-filled part of you to sit with you in order to be comforted and healed. Ask this part of you to speak out loud her feelings, her fears and her emotions. Let her words come through you as you sit in the position of the inner child. Ask her to tell you what happened, how it made her feel, and what she needed at that time. She may cry, scream, shake or completely break down. Allow her to be fully open to express her pain without holding back. Invite her to elaborate on why she still feels so bad. Is there a sense of injustice that the adults around her at the time were not responsive? Is she angry that she had to deal with something that a child should not?

Remember that emotions are energy in motion: they have a message to communicate. Your intention is to allow the emotion its rightful time and space to be heard, acknowledged and healed. While we may feel that we should be over the pain of childhood drama because we're adults now, the unprocessed emotional energy may still be trapped in your body and brain. It's time to release it and transmute it into healing energy.

If you forced yourself to "grow up," stay silent or "suck it up" for the sake of not causing a fuss or being embarrassed, you haven't allowed the emotion to flow.

You may have suppressed the emotion in order to cope and get on with life. On the other hand, perhaps you did communicate your pain but the adults in your life either didn't believe you, shamed you for speaking up, or didn't take action to help you. In this case the pain may still be simmering inside of you. Blocked or unacknowledged emotion will not stay silent forever. And all of the positive affirmations in the world won't convince your inner child that you are worthy and lovable.

As you let the emotion flow you may want to wrap yourself in a blanket, hold a soft pillow or wrap yourself in a self-hug to soothe your inner child. When you feel that she has communicated a good deal of what's been hurting for so long, you can switch chairs or imagine that you're now speaking from your adult self. Reassure your inner child that you are now her protector and friend; you won't judge her harshly and you will not leave her. Tell your younger self how much you appreciate her bravery and courage to be open. Let her know that you're sorry she has carried the pain for so long. (You're not accepting blame in this case. You are simply offering compassion by acknowledging how bad it must have felt to stay silent, to feel unimportant or unloved.)

You can ask the inner child if there is more to explain or share. Switch positions again and let her express any other emotion she wants to. Continue this process until you feel that the source of the pain has been identified and that from your adult position you've communicated how you will support, comfort and defend your inner child from this point forward. Continue to bathe yourself in soothing loving tones of support and compassion.

At the end of this process you may feel drained, exhausted, and tired. This is normal. Take the rest of the day to be quiet and calm. Do something that you really enjoy or find nurturing, such as a warm bath, watching a good movie, listening to music or reading a book. When you're able, write down what you learned from this dialogue in your journal.

This type of a process can also be enacted by imagining someone who hurt you or let you down in the past. Getting out the anger, rage, disappointment for what happened and by saying what you wished they would have done can help your wounded inner child get past the resentment and pain. Ultimately, we all must release the past with forgiveness and compassion to be truly free in the present.

Build A Compassionate Image

Dr. Paul Gilbert, creator of Compassionate Mind Training, offers workshop attendees a special exercise to help build a compassionate image to nurture and comfort us. I find that imagining an internal loving, compassionate figure such as a grandmother, wise elder, the Buddha, Christ, or an angel can be helpful if we find it hard to be compassionate toward ourselves. Dr. Gilbert explains that the image is really your own personal ideal, a being you would really appreciate feeling cared for and cared by. His suggestion is to give your compassionate image certain positive qualities such as the traits of wisdom, strength, warmth and non-judgment.

Allow yourself to imagine what the compassionate figure would look, sound, or feel like. Would it be a person, animal, saint, or a loved one from your past? What sort of vocal quality does this being have? How would you like for him or her to relate to you? How would you like to relate to your compassionate figure? Would you be silent and receive love, wisdom, and comfort? Or would you cry out to this figure, ask for help, or vent your feelings?

Imagine the types of phrases you would hear from your compassionate image. Perhaps elements of the loving-kindness Mettā meditation are appropriate. Your internal compassion companion may say, "I am here for you. May you be peaceful. May you not suffer. I will be here for you always. I wish you true happiness."

When you practice the safe place visualization described earlier in this chapter, you may wish to invite your compassionate figure to join you there to provide you with unconditional love and comfort.

I endured so many years of internal abuse and criticism from the "Supreme Court Judges" in my head that compassion seemed like what I needed most when I was feeling like a failure or when I beat myself up for not being perfect. But at times, I actually have found a fierce and feisty voice inside me that helps me assert myself or establish strong boundaries of protection. Sometimes an inner bully can actually be on our side.

From the darkness to the light, enter a character that is not for everyone…

The "F**k-You" Girl

As we process painful emotions, in addition to a compassionate figure, it may helpful to bring forward assertive, empowering aspects of our personality. Many of the clients who participated in my IOP for binge eating disorder tapped into anger as they examined the underlying cause for becoming self-critical and shaming. Some, who had endured abuse or neglect, found that after the need to be heard and soothed was met, they were able to voice extreme anger and disgust toward their caretakers, the perpetrator of their abuse, or the situation. While some found that anger made them vengeful, others found the feeling of anger prompted them to be more assertive in the present. Having practiced self-compassion and feeling more supported, they could now turn their energy toward appropriate self-care.

Turning what could be seen as destructive energy and making it useful, I often find that it helps to unleash an inner "F-you girl." Once the inner critic has settled down, we can still protect ourselves with an aspect of the self that is sometimes irreverent, aggressive, or edgy. Part of becoming resilient involves becoming assertive and sometimes that involves firing off a few F-bombs. Now I am not one to curse indiscriminately, but the word fu*k does have a certain power to it. Instead of "fuck you," your inner F-you girl may say "forget you." Either way, the intention is to take a stand for what we believe in and silence the haters (which are sometimes just figments of our own imagination!).

As we become champions and protectors of our inner child or judged self, sometimes we need to know that a strong internal persona really has our back — especially if the adults or authority figures in our lives weren't there for us. For me, my inner f-you girl has specific criteria for launching an f-bomb into the air. In fact, her criteria includes five Fs, which are tied to what really matters in my life. When faced with fear of criticism she reminds me that no one should really be set up as a judge to decide my fate, determine what I wear, how I behave, or where I go. Then she runs through the five Fs to be sure. When evaluating whether to pay attention to someone or my imagined critics, her inner dialogue sounds like this: "Are you 1) feeding me, 2) f**king me, 3) furthering my cause/business, 4) the father of my children or 5) a whole lotta fun? If not, get the "f" out of my face!"

Yes, I know this could seem a bit harsh or hostile — especially from me! But I found that my inner target needed some strength and fire to prevent me from backing down or giving in to conformity or not acquiescing to my true desires. So, in addition to my inner compassion figure, I've got an inner F-you girl. She rarely comes out or speaks up for more than a moment or two. And her conversation generally stays in my head. But if I'm particularly stressed or threatened, she may step up and be heard. I'm not always proud of her outbursts, but I admit that the tender part of me that has previously felt afraid to speak up now feels protected.

***

Once you've processed the hurt and trauma, and after you've launched a few F-bombs to utilize the positive side of drama, it's time to wipe the slate clean with a good dose of forgiveness. No matter how you were wounded, whether you were neglected, abused or gave away your power, or simply received painful blows from life, there comes a point where you've got to move past the pain and move into positivity.

Forgiving yourself for any mistakes you've made and offering forgiveness to those who may have done you wrong is essential to moving into the next phase of life mastery.

Forgiveness Meditation

It's obvious that we will have a hard time being fully present and appreciative of the life we have, if we're holding a grudge for some silly comment or serious assault we endured. Whether it was an error we made, or a misunderstanding from the past that still hasn't been resolved, we all know that carrying anger around or secretly wishing for vengeance will keep the heart closed and stem the flow of joy. To give yourself and others a break, so that you can move on, I highly recommend that you practice some form of forgiveness meditation.

My favorite version of the forgiveness meditation, for oneself and others, is adapted by one taught by Jack Kornfield, Buddhist teacher, meditation master, and author of *Meditation for Beginners* and *The Art of Forgiveness, Lovingkindness and Peace*. In this practice, we are asked to bring to mind situations where we have been hurt *and* times when we have done the hurting, whether to ourselves or to others.

I find that recognizing that everyone suffers and everyone has the power to cause suffering makes it easier to open up our heart to forgiveness and compassion. Through this practice we are able to recognize that due to our ignorance, pain, and suffering we make hurtful mistakes in the same ways that others do. It is therefore a kindness we offer to ourselves as well as others to forgive them so that in letting go of anger and blame, they, like us, can grow and evolve.

To begin the Forgiveness Meditation, go to a quiet, safe place and take slow deep breaths to become calm and centered. Begin by directing your forgiveness to other people by saying inwardly or out loud:

"There are many ways that I have hurt and harmed others. Whether knowingly or unknowingly, out of my pain, fear, anger, and confusion. I have betrayed or abandoned them and caused them suffering."

Bring to mind and visualize the ways you've hurt other people. Allow yourself to see and feel the pain you've caused out of your own pain, fear, and confusion. Get in touch with the sadness and regret inside of you. Know that if you choose to, you can let go of this burdensome pain and ask for forgiveness. Picture each situation that still weighs heavily on your heart. And then to each person you harmed, in your mind, repeat:

"I ask for your forgiveness, I ask for your forgiveness."

Because we are also hard on ourselves, with negative self-talk, criticism, and even self-punishment, it is useful to consciously receive forgiveness for yourself. As you consider the ways that you've hurt yourself, get in touch with the regret, sadness, and shame, and repeat these phrases:

"There are many ways that I have hurt and harmed myself, both knowingly and unknowingly. I have betrayed or abandoned myself many times through thought, word, or deed."

Recognizing the weight of the grief, sorrow, and blame you've carried, be willing to let go of the burdensome emotions and extend forgiveness for each of them in turn. Repeat to yourself:

"For the many ways I have hurt myself through action or inaction, out of fear, pain and confusion, I now extend a full and heartfelt forgiveness. I forgive myself, I forgive myself."

Naturally, we want to release others from the poisonous darts of blame we may shoot at them in our minds. So, we also extend forgiveness to those who have harmed us. Bring to mind the many ways you've been hurt or disappointed by other people. Allow yourself to picture and remember these many ways. Let the sadness and grief come to the surface and repeat the following:

"There are many ways that I have been harmed by others, abused, or abandoned, knowingly or unknowingly, in thought, word or deed."

Feel the sorrow you've carried from these situations and do yourself the great service of letting this burden of pain fall away by granting them forgiveness to the extent that you are ready. Then repeat the following:

"I now remember the many ways others have hurt or harmed me and wounded me out of their fear, pain, confusion and anger. I have carried this pain in my heart too long. To the extent that I am ready, I offer them forgiveness. To those who have caused me harm, I offer you my forgiveness, I forgive you."

Reclaiming your power

Each of the practices in this chapter are about healing, detoxing from destructive emotions and thought patterns so that you can move forward with confidence. True power comes from being conscious of the choices you are making in the present. Aligning your life choices with your heart-based values and acting in alignment with your true desires is the most authentic use of free will and the power which is inherently yours to use.

In Part III, we will take this power and put it to use by consciously setting up your life and relationships in ways that allow you to show up and thrive as your Authentic Self.

PART III

THRIVE: LIVE WHO YOU ARE

The Cornerstone Process
Step 3 — Accountability

Can I take responsibility for my life circumstances and transformation process?

From self-acceptance we move to the third step in laying in the foundation for true self-love: **Accountability**. Once we learn how the human mind is structured and programmed, we find it easier to forgive ourselves, our parents, and other "programmers" and recognize that going forward, it's up to us to create a life we love. Having learned that our past was riddled with a host of unconscious influences, we use our newfound awareness to act *consciously*. Accountability shifts the ownership and stewardship of our lives back to us. This can be terribly frightening and tremendously freeing.

Having accepted who you are, you are now free to create a written description of the *you* that you desire or intend to be. You may consider this your ideal Self, if you like. This version of you may not be perfect or flawless, but it lives an authentic life attuned to the energy of love and is fully aligned with your personal values, motivations, and ideals.

In Step 3, you'll explore the process of taking personal responsibility for your life without guilt, shame or pity parties and move on to creating a life you'll love. I do realize that for some people, it can be scary to think that we can no longer assign blame to our parents, past abusers, society, or religion. Just realizing that your future is your total responsibility may fill you with a heavy sense of dread. But know this, **you can**

and will get past this fear. And soon, you will re-experience the childlike wonder and joy of having a world of possibilities open to you.

Whatever you've felt hindered from doing can now be explored without fear of judgment, guilt, or shame. Your life can suddenly be lived with no one to answer to, seek approval from, or beg for permission. From this point on, your life is your own and you are accountable to your true Self *only*. And don't worry, you're not going to become a self-indulgent, hedonistic brat. You'll simply become more confident with your Authentic Self at the helm of your life.

5

Take Accountability for Your New Life

Now that you have uncovered your spiritual DNA, identified your values and acknowledged how you can achieve great and meaningful things, including your peak experiences, you'll now combine the essential ingredients of your true personality with your renewed personal power to take accountability for your life.

When accountable to someone for something, you are responsible for that action and you must be prepared to justify your actions to that person. In this case, **you must become accountable to yourself first and foremost.**

Taking accountability means reclaiming your authority as the author of your own heroic life story. And that's what this chapter is all about. Integrating your personality, talents, and interests and aligning them with your spiritual desires for self-expression will help you create a future life worth living. Your attitude and mindset dictate your possibilities, not your past experiences. Now you will consciously choose to adapt your attitude and mindset to live with joy and fulfillment.

Make your progress visible

Accountability requires awareness. So, especially for this chapter, I recommend that you take notes in a journal to track and be mindful of your progress as you embrace and embody your Authentic Self. Acknowledge and celebrate your successes along the way by writing down the times that you are there for yourself, the self-care rituals you do, the times that you held firm on your boundaries, and the times that you have fun or feel lighter.

Seeing written reminders of how far you've come will provide you with proof of your power. And remember, you will no longer look to other people for recognition, approval, or validation. Your journal, your notes, your little gold sparkly stars are going to do all of that for you.

The first thing to write down is your intention to live as your Authentic Self. Write a bold statement of your commitment to yourself. You could use some of the Personal Success Mantras you wrote in the last chapter, too. I've included some examples for you here.

I am committed to living as my Authentic Self.

I am boldly going after my dreams.

My happiness depends on me.

I claim my right to joy, success and love.

I give #ZeroFucks to what haters or trolls say.

Notice these statements are filled with declarations of what I want and what my standards are. They are in positive, present tense, and they imply that I am in control of my life. These statements will become your life manifesto, a written document which outlines your values, intentions and views.

It's important to recognize that life is about the choices we make. Every choice you have made has had some sort of effect in your physical reality — from where you live, how you dress, how you speak, what career you chose, and with whom you associate. In the past, whether you consider your choices to have been good or bad, they were made based on your level of awareness and development at that time. And in the words of Maya Angelou, "When you know better, you do better."

So far, we have explored how the mind and our subconscious programming has set us on a path of conformity. Now that we are being set free from that prison, this is where the excitement begins. In this present moment, you are free to choose everything in your life based on your desires, values, and interests, always aligning with the purpose and meaning you believe will bring you fulfillment. No more blame and no more regret. You are in the position of authority now.

Until now, you likely have been living out a life story where you probably had little sense of control over the things that happened to you. All of that changes today.

The power to choose how your life unfolds is based on your identity. In this book I suggest you live according to your Authentic Self, not the ego-based self that was created reactively and through the coercive process of socialization. You move from being a victim of circumstance, unconsciously reacting to what life throws at you with a focus on basic survival, to becoming the conscious author or hero of an epic life story, architecting a life based on your values and desires.

I realize that moving from victim or reactor, to author and creator of your life, can be both scary and freeing at the same time. It's not uncommon to see doubt, fear, or resistance come up as you move into a new way of being. That's also a part of the human experience. But don't worry, I've got you covered there, too! In the next chapter you'll learn how to become a master of your energy and emotions. Trust me, it's worth your effort.

Your mental story dictates your outer reality

Our next order of business is to revisit your past to reframe anything that has previously made you feel like a victim. In my LifeWriting workshops for authors and speakers, I teach a powerful self-narrative process using the Hero's Journey as a framework. The workshop involves writing or rewriting the story of your life in a way that brings past experiences into a positive and empowering context, seeing yourself as the hero of your life story.

We all have a story. Whether you are consciously aware or not, you have an internal story about who you are, what you're capable of, what you deserve and why you ultimately feel driven to do what you do. Your story has high points, low points, turning points, and is full of characters and influences. It is your personal, autobiographical reconstruction of the past and your anticipated future. Sometimes we have several stories, the ones we tell others and the ones we tell ourselves. The story we tell ourselves is what we will explore, define and begin to rewrite today.

Narrative Therapy

Based on research dating from the 1980s to present day, psychologists have explained that we all form an identity by integrating our life experiences into an internalized, evolving story of the self, which provides us with a sense of unity and purpose in life. The research behind narrative identity explains that the ways we make sense of our lives, through the stories we tell about ourselves, influence everything. From our ability to take care of ourselves, to our physical health, on to our tendency to recover quickly or slowly from injury, illness or trauma and more, your story dictates, in many respects, your destiny.

Your story has been formed, in part, by the past experiences and outside influences we've been exploring in the first part of this book. Buried within your story are underlying beliefs and assumptions about your place in the world today and how you think your life will unfold tomorrow and into the future. Some of the aspects of our story are based in myth and superstition!

Often the stories that we carry from our past make us feel small, limited, unfixable or unlovable. While none of that is true, those internalized beliefs are like programs in the back of our minds which impact our physical and emotional wellbeing, influence the choices we make and even dictate how many attempts we will make to transform our lives in the present.

Within your story are a cast of characters, each with their own underlying motives and desires, and scenes in your story from your past, present and even your imagined future. And you are the lead character in your life story. Are you playing the part of a hero or victim?

The good news is that your story is not written in stone. If you're not happy with your life, you can change it. You have the power to take control of the script of your life story. In other words, you play a dual role of the actor and author of your life story. You have the power to choose to become the hero of an epic life. And you have the power to write the next chapters of your life as an inspiring tale of fulfillment, vitality, and joy. You get to choose your own adventure.

The LifeWriting process I describe in this chapter allows you to investigate the story you unconsciously tell yourself about yourself so that you can determine what you want to change, and what kind of person you will become to live the most inspired life possible. If there is something in your past which haunts you today or exerts a negative influence on your confidence, hope or belief, then you have unconsciously given it a dominant role in your story, which may be holding you back from a life of joy and freedom. You can change that.

If your past beliefs about yourself made you think you were weak, locked into a certain lifestyle or unable to grow beyond your physical circumstances, you will be inspired to learn that those beliefs can be erased and replaced with more accurate, flexible and inspiring beliefs. You may have assumed your identity to be based on your role, your looks, your grades or your accomplishments. Now that you understand that your identity is that of a creative spiritual being, rich with infinite potential, you can take on the identity that is more closely aligned to the ideal self, the self you aspire to be, your Authentic Self.

While the facts of your past are unchangeable, the way you perceive and react to them, the way you integrate them into your personal story is not. When we feel a need to make changes in our lives, we can rewrite or revise our personal story whenever we want to. It is an opportunity to reinvent ourselves, to begin again, and to live in new and different ways.

As a creative being, you also have the ability to rewrite your internal mindset program to be the most powerful, inspiring and motivating ever. As you consciously choose to become the author of your life story, and put the past into an empowering perspective, you will gain the motivation to live with purpose and passion. This LifeWriting process can even lead to the resolution of longstanding health problems, relationship dysfunction and challenges in achieving success. An in-depth review of the scientific literature proves that this form of therapy is as effective as antidepressants or cognitive behavioral therapy.

You can read the stories of some of the coaches, healers and other Lightworkers who've been through The LifeWriting program by visiting www.MyLifeRewritten.com. Their stories of triumph will inspire you!

Put your past into an empowering context

Write the story of your life

It is helpful to think of your life story as a book that is evolving, expanding and open to revision. As such, each chapter of your life can provide a peek into the meaning, values and dreams that underly who you think you are, and who you aspire to be. In this context, your life story is not just a biography of the facts and events of your life, it's about how you integrate those facts and events internally. It's about how you pick apart and analyze those events, and how you weave them back together to make meaning.

Your personal narrative becomes a form of identity, in which the things you choose to include in your story, and the way you tell it, can both reflect and shape who you are. A life story doesn't just say what happened: it says why it was important, and what it says about who you are, who you'll become, and what may happen next in your life adventure.

The LifeWriting process involves: identifying the chunks of time that are easily recognized (these will be called the chapters of your life); defining the events or moments that had a significant impact on you; recalling any characters involved (these could be people, pets, places); uncovering the past sense or meaning attached to those events; and providing new interpretations of the past beliefs which may have a more empowering perspective, pointing to a brighter future. The end result of the process is a written narrative that provides a self-description or identity of power and purpose.

You can get access to printable worksheets that are useful in this process by visiting www.RealSelf.love. An example of the worksheet is presented at the end of this section for you.

1. Your Life Chapters

You start the process in this way. Identify the significant chapters of your life by looking at the periods of time that create large segments of time, such as early childhood, middle childhood, teenage years, early adulthood, and so on. You can also categorize your life chapters based on the significant experiences that lasted for extended periods of time, such as: the years spent in treatment for a particular illness or disease, the years before your parents divorced, the period of time at university, the period you spent working at your first major job, etc.

2. **Your Timeline of Life Events**

Once you've identified the chapters of your life, you will now create a timeline of life events for each chapter. The timeline should include entries of general and specific events that stand out in your memory which had an impact on you in some way, the approximate dates of particular scenes of importance, the locations, any other people or characters that were involved, and the outcomes of the event. You don't have to list every little detail of your life, only the prominent scenes or events that may be impacting your sense of self and your ability to make change in the present.

TIMELINE OF LIFE EVENTS

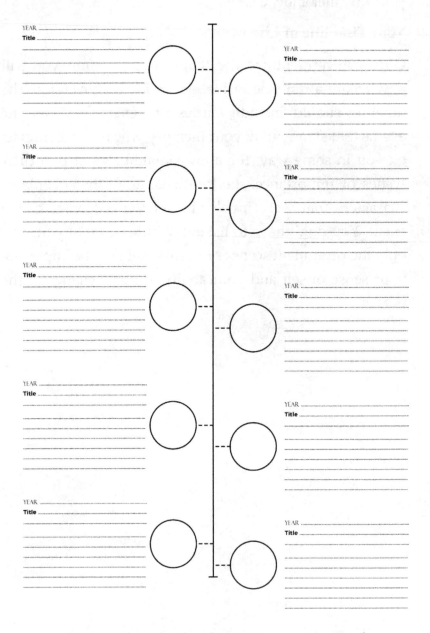

You can download and print your own copy of
the Life Event Timeline at www.RealSelf.love

3. New Interpretations

Next you look at the significant events in each chapter, and see what lessons were learned, what assumptions were made about your place in the world, what thoughts or beliefs got imprinted about how life works, what is assumed about other people, or what is possible for you.

Often you can see clearly how a particular event dramatically changed you or your course in life. You may finally recognize how an event shaped your sense of self-worth, or why you began to stay silent, why you don't trust people, why you look for others to rescue you, or why you stopped doing what you really wanted and instead began to put others' needs above your own. Seeing your events laid out on a timeline can help you see the course of your life with new insight.

Looking at the hidden meaning behind each event brings into your conscious awareness how they have shaped your beliefs, behavior and sense of self by answering these key questions:

✓ What's the impact of those beliefs on your life today?

✓ Have those hidden meanings influenced your decisions in a way that has served your survival but sentenced you to a limited way of being?

✓ What have those beliefs cost you?

✓ What is the potential impact of continuing with those beliefs? Will they get you to where you want to go?

✓ Are there any issues or repeating issues you can see now?

4. Life story themes

Next you will identify the overarching theme your life story has. Just as if you were describing a book's theme, what is the overall vibe of your life story? Is it a tragic story of loss, or a 'woe is me' tale of misery?

When it comes to the ultimate meaning of our stories, you may come to understand that it's all a matter of perspective and personality. If we look at families where multiple children grew up in the same conditions and had similar experiences, we are often surprised that they ended up with totally different outcomes. For example, there are many cases of children who grew up with an abusive parent where one child went on to become an abuser himself, while the other became a protector or rescuer type.

What accounts for this difference? It comes down to personality, temperament and mindset. While it is debatable whether we can change our personality or temperament (some research indicates these are fixed at birth and relatively stable over time), we can change our interpretation of events and our mindset about our ability to change our reactions.

We can decide what theme our life story takes on because though we cannot change the negative, hurtful or tragic things that happened in the past, we can take the lessons learned and positively use them as fuel to create a life of purpose and fulfillment. We can even transmute the pain of our past into a drive to help others. Rather than our identity being fixed, imprisoned or doomed by the negative experiences of our past we can be rise up, be redeemed, and reclaim our right to happiness.

Narrative psychologist Dan P McAdams, PhD, from Northwestern University in the United States, has done extensive research on narrative identity. And after conducting thousands of life story interviews, he uncovered common themes in the personal narratives of his research subjects. The main themes which correspond to positive life outcomes are stories of redemption: going from rags to riches, from sin to redemption, from illness to recovery, surviving to thriving. And within those themes, when we are able to look at our role in life as one of the conscious agent of choice, rather than the reactive actor, we begin to realize greater control over our life story.

As you gain insight into your past and how it has shaped you, it is possible to find a new sense of coherence or meaning in your life. That, too, is a sign that you are moving toward greater psychological wellbeing. Life is no longer seen as a random combination of negative events; it has a sense of continuity, leading you somewhere.

The story themes of redemption mentioned above allow us to craft a positive identity where we are in control of our lives, we are loved, and we see that we are moving through life with a sense that whatever obstacles we encounter can been redeemed by positive outcomes. Dr. McAdams refers to these as generative stories. His research found that when people recall and narrate important life events that follow a redemption sequence, where a negative scene turns positive, or when experiences of suffering or setback eventually lead to positive, growth-inducing outcomes, then we as adults can see our lives as heroic tales of transformation. We can even see how our past set us up to make a difference in the lives of others, allowing us to turn our most painful life lessons into blessings.

The redemption story is seen in stark contrast to the theme of contamination where one feels that they started off pure or innocent, and life events unfolded in dark, sinister ways that contaminated their purity and goodness. Research shows that contamination stories are linked to more depression and anxiety, and less hope for a brighter future.

5. **Write your life story**

In our LifeWriting workshops, we invite participants to write stories based on their entire lives, or a few chapters of their lives. While often these are intended to be published in a book to provide inspiration to others, for this exercise you can keep the story to yourself. It is part of your self-discovery and healing process, and it's best to write without fear of anyone else reading it.

Writing your life story is meant to set the stage for how you will live from this point forward. For this exercise, you are invited to focus on gleaning all of the positive meaning from the past so that your story becomes one of redemption, growth, inspiration for yourself and others.

Looking over the past chapters of your life, choose a few important scenes and write a story that brings you forward to today. I suggest you include a detailed account of one of your happiest memories in life or a peak experience, a sad memory in life, a low point or disappointment in life, a turning point in life and a future vision of what you think the next chapter of life will be like. I suggest you write the story with you playing a more heroic role. In the last chapter of this book, we will help you make that future vision come true!

This LifeWriting process is so therapeutic that I joined forces with a brilliant Jungian therapist to expand the workshops to include archetype discovery work. If you're interested in joining us for a live workshop or online course, check out www.MakeYourMarkGlobal.com.

Who are you now?

Look over the paradigms of possibility and Personal Success Mantras that you wrote in Chapter 2, and the personal story you wrote in the exercise above. The paradigms of possibility and Personal Success Mantras can be used to describe who you are now, and who you aspire to be as you let this transformation fully run its course.

What is the vision for your current life or future healthy relationships? Is there a driving mission or motivating intention that you want to bring forth in your life such as starting a new business, or getting your body healthy, or moving to a new place? What do you really hope to bring to the world through your self-expression? And if you had to describe yourself with several adjectives, sprinkle those throughout your own life manifesto.

Collect the powerful statements, mantras and themes to create a collage of beautiful text, colors, or images that really speak to you and inspire you. This exercise is similar to the Brand Identity mood boards we create for clients, which at a glance, provide insight and inspiration for what the brand or personality stands for. They evoke emotion and stimulate feelings.

Your collage could also be become your own personal manifesto, like the one I created for the Real Self Love Movement seen below. Be creative as you illustrate what your core beliefs are. Write personal "I am" statements about yourself to describe what you deserve and desire in life.

I LOVE YOU, Me!

REAL SELF LOVE IS MY
BIRTHRIGHT

I ALIGN MY MIND,
BODY, SOUL AND
SPIRIT FOR PEACE

I am united with all love

I CHERISH MY BODY
EMBRACE MY SHADOW
DEFINE MY DESTINY
CHOOSE HAPPINESS

I AM FREE
TO EXPRESS MYSELF
WHOLEHEARTEDLY

I am a virtuous being

I CLAIM MY RIGHT TO
JOY, SUCCESS AND LOVE

I LIVE IN AN
ATTITUDE OF
GRATITUDE

I am the architect of my life

I AM BOLDLY GOING
AFTER MY DREAMS.
I AM CONSCIOUSLY
LIVING MY PURPOSE.

NOW
is my time to
RISE

I AM PERFECT,
WHOLE AND COMPLETE

w w w . R e a l S e l f . L o v e

You can download and print your own copy of
the Real Self-Love Manifesto at www.RealSelf.love

Visualize your future

As you take accountability for the life that you will live from this day forward, the future vision of you living as your most empowered and Authentic Self can be reinforced using this visualization meditation process. Taking guidance from the general future life you wrote about in the last exercise, you will now imagine a specific day in the life of the future you.

Move to a quiet place and get comfortable. Maybe brew a nice cup of tea, or light some candles and put on some soft or funky music. Get into a mood that feels inspired and relaxed. I want you to imagine a day in the life of your boldest, most confident Authentic Self. You can write down your future vision and then imagine it as you meditate, or speak it into your Smartphone or a recording program on your computer. (I've recorded a guided visualization audio that you can listen to before or during this exercise. Visit www.RealSelf.love)

Imagine the perfect morning as your perfect ideal self. From the moment that you wake up, what are you feeling? Where are you? Who's with you? As you imagine yourself as this future, bold, beautiful you, what do you do when you first wake up? How do you feel? Are you alone or with your beloved? Do you wake up bubbling with enthusiasm to go to work? Or is this kind of a happy vacation day where you get to snuggle in and snooze a little longer. Is someone is serving you breakfast in bed?

Just imagine the perfect day as you wake up as your ideal self. And from the moment that you get out of bed, what do you do next? Do you make breakfast for you and your family?

Do you put on your running shoes or yoga clothes and get some exercise? Or do you enjoy a cup of tea while writing in your journal? Are you meditating? Whatever you do before the day really gets into full swing, write down or speak into your recorder; what you would do when you wake up at your best, as your ideal Authentic Self.

I really want you to put yourself into those moments. How does it feel? How does it look? What do you see around you? What do you smell? What do you taste?

Next, do you go away to work? Do you work at home? Do you work at all? If you're on vacation, what's next in your morning?

Then imagine what happens at lunch time as your perfect divine self when you are free to choose your life. How do you spend the midday? Write it down or speak it out. And try to imagine it in full Technicolor with all the sights and sounds and sensations.

So, what happens during the rest of the day and your evening? Do you meet up with friends? Do you come home for dinner with your beloved or with your family? Imagine your perfect end of the day.

And then as you transition into evening, how does that play out for you? Really get specific about the type of person that you'd like to be on a day-to-day basis.

In Chapter 6, we'll take the next steps into finding the action plan and creating and architecting every aspect of your ideal, "Diamond" life.

Authentic Self-Expression

Another way I encourage you to become confident in nurturing yourself and to move beyond old adaptive ways of functioning, is to tap into your authentic talents, gifts and strengths. Rather than continuing as a wounded, traumatized, or "recovering" person, my training and experience with positive psychology has shown me time and again that living from our strengths is a surefire way to ignite our fire for authentic living.

Authentic, creative self-expression is a guiding principle I teach in my retreats and workshops. Once we write paradigms of possibility, Personal Success Mantras, write our life stories from positive perspectives, and design our life manifestos, we make an agreement to live these messages daily for the rest of our lives.

Only you can tell if you are stretching, growing, and fully embracing your Authentic Self. There is no external judge or jury. You are now accountable to yourself and yourself alone. Take it seriously, as if your life depends on it. Because it does!

Authentic Self Accountability

Once you've declared what you stand for and what you're aiming for in life, it's time to hold yourself accountable to those principles. Before we even think of outlining major goals and life plans, we've got to be clear about who's in charge. If you are your own boss, then you need to hold yourself accountable to your vision and standards.

If you were an employee and the boss needed to evaluate your performance against those standards, how would you do?

Well, now consider that *you are* your own boss. Each week, evaluate yourself to determine how well you're living in accordance with your values.

Check in weekly to ask yourself:

- Did I do my best to express my Authentic Self? (Or was I hiding on the sidelines, not expressing my opinions or not being actively involved in life?)

- Was I focused on my future vision and major growth areas for the year? (Or was I distracted by, or entangled in, other people's goals and visions?)

- Was I consciously and boldly taking action toward my dreams? (Or was I mindlessly watching streaming TV series, scrolling through social media posts, or being "busy" with chores?)

Being accountable is about claiming responsibility for the choices you make and the way that your life is turning out. Once you've gotten comfortable with this kind of Authentic Self-evaluation, then it's best for you to write your own self-description. Like your Personal Success Mantras from Chapter 2, your personal manifesto can provide the fuel to tune out the haters (both real and imagined). It can also give focus and direction to your architecting your ideal life.

Now let's get even more audacious and ambitious and amp up your positivity meter so that you can design the blueprint for your epic life. It's time to become a master of your emotions and energy, and then the architect of your Diamond Life.

6

Master Your Energy & Emotions

According to Taoist philosophy and Chinese medical practice, one can and *should* become master of their life force energy to enjoy optimal wellbeing of body, mind, spirit, environment and relationships. We can do this by living in harmony with the natural energy of Life.

In Eastern philosophy, they describe life force energy as 'qi' in Chinese, 'ki' in Japanese, and as prana in Hindu traditions. This vital energy flows through the sky, the earth, our bodies and our minds naturally. Where this energy flows, life flourishes. When this life force energy flows harmoniously through all of our body's channels, called meridians, we can remain healthy and vital for a long life, and we can quickly recover from illness, injury, shock or trauma. The Chinese have documented the ability to masterfully manipulate, collect and transmit this life force energy for thousands of years, and now is the time for you to master it as well.

Normally, our qi, the precious life sustaining energy, flows through our bodies in a balanced, harmonious way. This energy nourishes all of our tissues and organs and even supports our mental and emotional wellbeing. When faced with an illness, infection or injury, our life force energy is normally distributed in such a way as to bring the body back into balance, wholeness and vitality. We can bounce back from our illnesses, surgery and diseases easily, quickly and completely when our qi is abundant and in flow.

Our vital life force energy can become stuck or sluggish as a result of not living in harmony with our natural energy flow. For example, not eating healthy food, drinking too much alcohol, or engaging in unhealthy behaviors, relationships and even careers can cause our energy to become depleted or stagnant. When this happens, we experience dis-ease. We may become sick, tired or depressed and devoid of joy or passion.

I'm sure that I don't have to remind you of just how miserable life can be when we drift away from our true sense of self, and how limited we can feel when we are compelled to follow the crowd, society, or families. So now that you've rediscovered who you really are and you're more accepting of your true nature, it's time to give you tools to manage your energy and use your emotions wisely so you can live on your own terms for the rest of your life. To live your life in alignment with your values and desires, you're going to need to learn how to tap into your own wisdom, intuition, and internal guidance system, as well as know when to seek answers from wise, trusted sources.

To avoid getting sidetracked and overpowered by feelings of being overwhelmed by stress, confusion, or doubt, it's time to learn how to integrate all of the mindfulness, compassion and acceptance elements you've learned so far into your everyday life. In addition to committing to a regular self-care routine, in this chapter we will explore some powerful, proven techniques for mindfully managing emotions and regulating your energy so you feel more flow, fulfillment, and personal power. This will help to protect your overall well-being, relationship harmony, and keep you on track to achieve your goals.

To begin, it's helpful to understand that everything in our universe is made up of energy and information. This is also true of our physical body. If we skim the surface of a quantum physics textbook, we discover that we're all connected via a web of electromagnetic energy. Our bodies and brains are made of electromagnetic energy and it is the management of this energy which is important to master. Our thoughts, intentions, and attention can influence the energy of our bodies and even the world around us. Our thoughts are so powerful that with sufficient emotional energy behind them, they can directly influence material reality.

While some people refer to this as the Law of Attraction, it's helpful to realize that this "law" is actually part of a larger set of rules that govern our entire universe (so far as we can study it.) So, don't go thinking that I'm drifting off into the land of new age, woo-woo pseudoscience here. The energy and emotional management techniques outlined here are based in science.

It's pretty clear what happens to us when our energy is low or chaotic. We can't concentrate, we give into temptation (such as with food, sex, or alcohol), we become more argumentative, or we withdraw and sulk. When our energy is high, we tend to look at life through a positive lens. We are easily motivated to get up and get going and we're interactive, fun, and kind to others.

The Anatomy of Your Energy Body

The good news is that we can learn how to tune into the energy field of the universe — tapping into energies near and far — to bring forth what we need for our wellbeing at any given moment. We can also learn to interpret our inner emotional energy to bring forth wisdom, motivation, or peace. So, before we move into the final stages of the Cornerstone Process, I want to empower you with techniques to keep you riding high emotionally and energetically. Becoming the master of your life force energy begins with understanding your body's subtle energetic anatomy.

When you want to manifest anything new in your life, the goal is to bring *all* of you into alignment. That is, get yourself into a state of harmony and congruence, where there is no conflict between your physical energy, your thoughts, and your emotions. This will empower you to create positive change in your physical health, your inner sense of wellbeing, the outer world, and your relationships. Your thoughts, emotions and physical body each have an associated energetic component that can be influenced in many ways.

Rigorous scientific investigation of the energy fields around the human body has been very limited, until now. For Westerners, it's hard to measure and study what you cannot see. But this is changing. We can now read excellent reports on Russian research into the Kirlian phenomenon of energy discharges around plants and animal organisms and humans in *Galaxies of Life* (1973). These energy emanations can be recorded by a process known as Kirlian photography.

With the wider acceptance of acupuncture, reflexology and acupressure, people can now *feel* the subtle energy that flows in their body. With a variety of hands-on and energy healing modalities like qigong and therapeutic touch, we are seeing resolution of physical problems. We've made a great deal of progress in our understanding of what Eastern cultures have known for thousands of years.

Your subtle body

Surrounding your physical body are energy fields which we can now measure via electrical sensing devices — think of electro encephalograms or EEG machines which measure brain waves. But this only represents a fraction of the energy that makes up your essence. According to the spiritual philosophy of Hinduism, when we die what leaves the body at death is a ball of subtle, invisible energy that vibrates at a higher rate than the physical body. This energy ball is referred to as the subtle body, and it consists of several layers or sheaths. According to Patañjali, the renowned Hindu sage and medical scholar of several Sanskrit texts, one of which is responsible for modern day yoga, the sheathes around the body are energy fields encoded with information.

Most people refer to the collection of energy sheathes surrounding the body as the **aura**, which is believed to be made of up at least 7 energy fields that serve different and distinct functions while we are alive, occupying a physical body.

It's often helpful to consider the layers of the aura like the famous Matryoshka dolls, also known as Russian nesting dolls. The popular set of wooden dolls of decreasing size are placed one inside another. The outer wooden doll, which separates, top from bottom, to reveal a smaller figure of the same sort inside, which has, in turn, another figure nested inside of it, and so on.

According to the *Tibetan Book of the Dead*, when you die, there are three layers of the energy body that lift off in sequence at the moment of death. Understanding the makeup of these 3 layers of energy fields is essential to your mastery of your life, which is what we'll explore in this chapter.

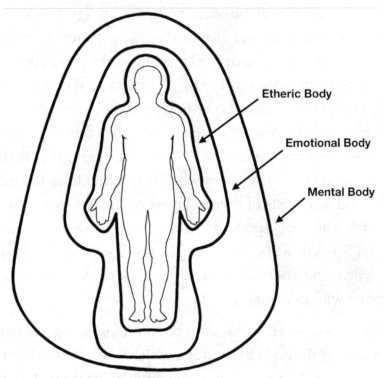

Etheric Body

Emotional Body

Mental Body

The Subtle Body: 3 Inner Layers of the Aura

The Mental Body: In the death process, the first energy layer to lift off is the mental body, which is the outer layer which carries imprinted thoughts. This is a very broad energy field and is the most subtle of the three. Located in the mental body are all the most powerful mental contents or fixed thoughts. These thoughts may be conscious or unconscious and can radically influence an individual's overall life patterns or self-image. For example, thoughts like, "I'll never make it." Or, "Don't trust people" may be lodged in the mental body. Some believe these may be the residues of negative past life experiences.

The Emotional Body: Next the emotional body goes, which is the energy field that carries the imprinted, embedded feelings. Sometimes called the astral body, this energy field adheres closely to the physical body and extends of about two to four feet away from us. The emotional body is the layer where the remnants of feelings from past events remain. These feelings may be grief, anger, disappointment, apathy, etc. Physically, this energy level is denser than the mental body and it may be strongly affected by negative thoughts from the mental body. When its feeling contents become highly charged and not released, it will affect the lower etheric energy body adversely. Like the mental body, feelings from past lives may be stuck here, too.

The Etheric Body: Finally, the level of energy closest to the physical body is the etheric body, which is often referred to as the vital body or life energy body. This energy body is well known to healers and acupuncturists and can be seen and sensed by some people. The etheric body is the most dense of the three subtle bodies and is physically perceptible to many people as heat emanating from parts of the body. It radiates out from the physical body about one to two inches and is the field worked within therapeutic practices like acupuncture, shiatsu, therapeutic touch and hands-on healing.

This field surrounds the body most closely and could be called "the physical memory field" because it carries all the painful subtle memory traces or imprints of physical trauma, whether lesions, fractures, tumors, amputations, wounds or diseases. In the Yoga Sutras, the leftover traces of trauma that Patañjali calls the *klesas* or "sufferings" are said to be carried by the subtle body.

In medical terms, there is a well-known example of how a residual memory of trauma can be held in the etheric body, a painful phenomenon known as "phantom limb" pain often experienced by amputees. In similar fashion, when things are lodged in the etheric body at the time of death in a past life, they can be experienced in this life. Repressed feelings from the emotional body may remain stuck at the etheric level to produce organic problems in the physical body.

During my training in acupuncture, I became fascinated by our ability to tap into this etheric energy field via needling or applying pressure to specific points on the body. Later, with investigation into past life regression therapy, I was blown away by the recognition that many of my patients had what could be considered irrational fears, phobias, or limiting beliefs that completely blocked their healing process. I began to see clearly how these problems were caused by traumas they endured earlier in life.

Further, when I began coaching and mentoring speakers and authors who aspire to share their work with a wider audience, I was confronted by patterns of self-sabotage and unexplained 'illnesses' that would come up just before a performance or on-camera appearance. Beyond the normal human fear of judgment when going on stage or on air, I found that many of my clients could articulate a primal fear that they consider to be left over traumatic residues of past lives.

Some have found through past life regression sessions that they were killed or tortured in past lives because of their controversial beliefs or special abilities. Some regression stories involved having witnessed people being burned at the stake or tragically unjustly persecuted and they did nothing to stop it. As a result, at the time of death there were beliefs locked into their subtle bodies which traveled with them beyond death. These show up and create problems in this life.

My clinical experience has shown evidence that our emotions, thoughts and traumatic injuries can be locked into these energy fields, making the traditional and holistic treatments like talk therapy, surgery, acupuncture, massage, osteopathy and nutritional intervention only partially helpful. We could treat some symptoms, bringing some relief with these modalities, but often the results wouldn't last. This understanding of the subtle body layers helped me understand why.

Clearing the Subtle Bodies of Present and Past Life Experiences

Understanding a bit of how the three subtle bodies or energy fields affect each other, it is often quite easy to see how a heavy thought hanging around the mental field can influence feelings within the emotional field. For example, the leftover unconscious thought "I'm a failure" can easily create nagging feelings of depression. Knowing how feelings can negatively influence the energy or vitality of the physical system by depressing the etheric field, we see people who feel tired all the time. That in turn can lead to overall low energy which can manifest physically as poor appetite, shallow or constricted breathing, heart pains, or other forms of depletion.

I'm not here to persuade you to believe in reincarnation, but I do believe that whether from this life or a previous one, there are thoughts, emotions and physical issues that get locked into our cells — our auras — and they can get triggered, causing us to shut down, become ill or otherwise self-destruct. We all carry major unconscious imprints where we have suffered a physical accident or trauma from this life. I've seen that despite visiting the most skilled therapists, trying the most effective physical or nutritional interventions and even undergoing surgical operations, if all three levels of our subtle body have not been 'cleared' and are not taken into account, there is often reversion to the earlier pattern.

If you feel that you are being impacted by deep memories that don't resolve easily with the practices outlined in this book, I invite you to consider the Deep Memory Regression Process, created by Roger Woolger, Holotropic Breathwork created by Stanislav and Christina Grof, or Dreamtime Healing with Holographic Kinetics technique taught by Steve Richards. Visiting their respective websites will lead you to directories of people trained in these modalities that can help facilitate the release of trauma locked into your subtle bodies.

Now let's look at what you can do on your own to bring more energy and flow to your life by impacting the three layers of your energy body that have the greatest influence on your daily life. As we investigate what drives you on a daily basis, the three key areas of your energy that we want to keep in flow include your head, heart, and hara.

Your 3 Energy Centers

Head and Heart

You're probably already aware of our two strongest electromagnetic communicators, our brain and our heart. Measuring the power of brain waves on an electroencephalogram (EEG) and heart waves on an electrocardiogram (ECG) make it quite clear and visible. Without energy flowing from these two power centers, life as you know it would end.

Yet there is so much more the brain and heart do. The energy they emit directly influences our day-to-day experience, and in turn our ability to attract more abundance, vitality and joy into our lives. Have you heard anyone say, "I'm stuck in my head" or "I follow my heart"? Without giving those words much attention, you may not realize just how true they are.

Researchers at the Institute of Heart Math explain that our heart is 5,000 times more powerful than our brain, and the electrical energy from the heart can be measured up to 20 feet away from our body. The heart's energy field has the shape of a torus, kind of like an elongated donut. This energy field is one aspect of the aura. Remember that of all the layers of the aura we have, there are three to focus our attention on: the physical (etheric), emotional, and mental. This is important because our experience of what happens in our lives is filtered through what is already held in our energy field.

This means if you hold resistant thoughts, beliefs, or grudges about someone or something you will see more of the same thing happening in your life, until you let it go. When you release old beliefs and clear stuck energy and get these key areas in balance or flow, you will see great shifts in your life experience.

The electrical field of your aura stores information, including every thought, belief, emotion, and experience you've ever had. Your aura can also be considered a two-way communication gateway between your physical body and everything outside of you that transmits and receives information.

Maybe you've noticed that you have recurring patterns in your life. For example, maybe you always attract a certain kind of romantic partner. You just seem to always meet a particular type of person — whether for your pleasure or pain. Many of my clients who've found themselves almost always in codependent, toxic relationships say that it happens so easily they think they must naturally attract these partners like nectar attracts bees.

Or perhaps you've known someone who seems to repeatedly come down with some illness or stress-induced breakdown. And while life can certainly put us at risk of sickness, in their case it appears as though they were silently calling in those circumstances. Like a computer operating system, the information field that makes up our aura codes for situations and tendencies that we are often unaware of.

You are a human antenna. Your body is constantly sending out and receiving signals from your head and heart.

Your aura influences the to and fro flow of messages sent and information received. Therefore, the data that is stored in your aura will impact your experience of life.

It's kind of like trying to tune a radio or television to a particular station when there is a wall interfering with the sound waves. The antenna simply won't receive the signal and the quality of the auditory output will be affected. You could also imagine that the beliefs, doubts and fears held in your energy space will impact what you attract into your life. This is why I spent so much time in the previous chapter providing you with ways to clean up the false or limiting beliefs, grudges, and self-criticism you may have held for years.

You may have noticed that life has kept sending you situations that matched those energy imprints. They often caused you to experience more relationships with critical partners or projects that failed, just to back up your belief that you were lame or incapable. As you've seen, the good news is that you have the power to change resistant thoughts and emotions and choose to replace them with ones that support you in transforming your life.

Hara

The hara describes the energy center below your belly button. In Chinese medicine and in qigong practice we call it the Dantien. The hara corresponds to the second and third chakra, so some describe it as the center of our sexual or primal energy. While your hara energy is not measured on an electrical device, we certainly know the impact of this area of our body.

If we are stressed, our hara is out of flow. In a fight or flight state, our body pumps out adrenaline and we may feel butterflies or knots in our stomach or get indigestion. In addition, the stress response decreases the release of the bonding hormone oxytocin. When that's low, our focus turns away from snuggling and being sexual into basic survival. In a lovey-dovey or affection state, the hara is turned on and we experience feelings we associate with love, sexuality, and feeling energized or motivated.

My colleague, Yvette Taylor, Founder of the Energy Alignment Method (EAM) and author of *The Ultimate Self-Help Book*, has created an energy psychology tool which is meant to help you get into a flow state so your energy can take you where you want to go in life. According to EAM, when you have all three working together, your head, heart, and hara, your life will be in flow. But that's just the beginning.

3 States of Energy Flow

Whether you are talking about a thought or an emotion, your physical health or a relationship, it really doesn't matter. Your energy will always be in one of three states: in flow, in resistance, or in reversal.

In Flow

When we talk about the state of being in flow, it means that your overall energy — including your head, your heart, and your hara — is in alignment. There is nothing in your aura which prevents you from manifesting your desires, and therefore there is no conflict in your energy. We describe this as being congruent and therefore sending out a matching energetic message.

Yvette likes to say that you know you're in flow when you have one of those days when everything is going great for you. You wake up feeling great. You find $5 on the ground. Someone opens the door for you, tells you that you look beautiful, and you feel inspired. You feel supported. Everything seems easy. It feels like the universe is on your side.

In Resistance

This is when your energy is not in alignment. There is some kind of energy battle going on between different parts of you. For example, your thoughts (head) are thinking one thing and your heart and hara are sending out an opposing message, which is conflicting. It could be there is something in your aura that contradicts your mental idea or desire, and therefore the energetic message you're sending is not congruent.

You would experience this as an internal tug of war or a push-pull battle within yourself. Some describe this as a stickiness, or a lack of momentum where you just can't seem to take action or maintain any forward movement. It's like being pulled in opposite directions, or having that annoying kid in the playground holding onto your hoodie as you try to get away. The good news is that it's just energy in resistance, which means it can be changed.

In Reversal

This is when your energy is moving in opposite directions. We say this means you're not at all in alignment, but in a sense they are. Each of your energy centers is sending out the same message; it's just not a positive one. Your head, heart, hara and aura are all in congruence that whatever experience is present, is bad.

This state is like an electrical shock. Usually, an energy reversal has occurred due to past experiences in this life (or past lives). It doesn't have to have been traumatic; it's likely it was just a situation in which you had no control. So, your energy did and continues to do what is needed to survive — it runs in the opposite direction, away from the thing it perceives is "wrong." This means it usually flows in the opposite direction of everything you think or say you want.

Think back over your last 24 hours. Can you identify any points when you were in these three states? The good news is that the Attunement Meditation and the Energy Alignment Method, which I am about to share with you here, both enable you to stop being in resistance or reversal, and change your energy to be in flow. Then you'll be primed and ready to manifest and co-create whatever you want in life. This is the critical piece required before I teach you how to design your Diamond Life.

The Attunement Meditation™

Nearly fifteen years ago, I developed a five-part mindfulness practice called the Attunement Meditation™. I have since taught it all over the world to thousands of people. It has proven to be a simple way for people to reap the benefits of the various meditation types I described in Chapter 4, including breath awareness, non-judgmental awareness, describing with words, loving-kindness, compassion, and gratitude.

The process is especially useful in times of stress or anxiety to bring you instant calm and peace. With regular and repeated practice, you can use it to build up positive emotions, compassion, and gratitude, as well become better attuned to your intuition and creativity. The five steps will impact your overall physiology and help to even enhance your intimate relationships.

The Attunement Meditation™ will help you bring balance to head, heart and hara and it will enable you to release resistance and remove energy reversals. What people love about The Attunement Meditation™ is that it helps them align with the field of universal love and compassion while focusing their attention on the thoughts, feelings, and aspirations they want to experience. Miracles become everyday occurrences. This magical force can be drawn upon and channeled to propel you toward your goals for a life full of joy, good health, and prosperity. It can also provide you with psychological insight on past traumas that allows you to clear their negative influences more easily.

The five steps are also aligned with the five stages of the Cornerstone Process. Here's how each of the five steps work.

Allow

Your initial step toward peace and authentic power in any situation is to ALLOW, to drop resistance, stop struggling, and cease fighting. It sounds counterintuitive, but when you stop fighting your emotions, disease, or circumstances, you open yourself up to greater power for transformation.

What if releasing the need to control your situation could increase your sense of personal power? Could it be that letting go of resistance to what is happening could ease your suffering? Could you let this moment be exactly as it is without fighting, struggling, or pushing toward a new direction? What would happen if you stopped trying to "fix" things?

I'm inviting you to allow the present moment to be exactly as it is — without judgment. This doesn't mean accepting it FOREVER, for all things are temporary. It helps to recite the mantra, "This too shall pass," and remember that there's no reason to resist this moment.

When you give a circumstance permission to be *as it is*, without making it wrong or bad, you'll be more open to the message of why and how you got there in the first place. You'll also be more open to innovative solutions. Have you heard the phrase, "what you resist, persists?" In this context, it's so true.

By surrendering to this moment, we allow all thoughts, judgments, and beliefs to rise and then fall away. God Consciousness, Divine Light or something not of this world shines through with wisdom, a plan, a perfect solution to all that troubles you.

"When we are no longer able to change a situation, we are challenged to change ourselves."

~Victor Frankl

When you can't change the situation, change your perspective.

Since the only thing you can change is you, ask yourself; "What if this situation stays the same and I change instead?" Consider this fully.

What could you change in yourself (or about yourself) that would make it easier for you to accept what's going on? You could change your attitude, opinion, or judgment that the situation is bad. What if you looked for what is good or right about it? What if you said, "This is good, and it can stay just as it is," and see what comes up for you. Just try it, to see what happens.

Of course, you could just continue along the path of resistance, thinking that you're right and the situation is just plain wrong! But where will that path lead you? Living in stress — and in denial — can lead to increased blood pressure, chronic fatigue, immune system collapse, lost libido and more. So, recognize that holding onto a perspective, attitude, or opinion about a situation or person only hurts you. You always have a choice in how you respond. And you always have the choice to leave a bad situation. This frees you up from the often foolish or heroic attempt to change others.

Allow for spontaneous resolutions to problems

Often when we give a situation or person the space to be as they are, the change we desire may come spontaneously. When we stop judging others harshly and adopt a more accepting mental posture, it's easier for others to find harmony and compromise.

The stressful situations we're so busy fighting often resolve completely all by themselves when we let go of our need to control them.

But whether that change comes or not is irrelevant. Your peaceful state of mind is of the greatest importance. When you are at peace, life has the opportunity to flow and unfold with natural ease and grace. So, instead of stubbornly holding onto a position with dogged determination, imagine that you decide to change your reaction to what's going on.

What if you said, "This has a right to be happening and I don't have to get upset"? Can you start to see where the power lies? You have the power to change your mind, the story, the interpretation, and your response. The mere act of saying "I can get upset or not" shifts the energy, ever so slightly, from dis-empowered frustration to mildly empowered strength. You still have the choice to get upset, if you desire. You're not taking away your right to respond; you're simply minimizing the negative effect of assuming that only one solution is best.

By simply shifting into a more allowing and accepting posture and mental attitude you may feel your tension decrease. The more you let go of the position of "me" against the situation, the more you feel negative energy decrease. When negativity can be replaced by neutrality, things settle down to a happy medium. Then you may have new insights on how to resolve the situation in a way you didn't even consider before.

Personal peace is one decision away

Can you at least glimpse the possibility of allowing your life situations to be, without trying to fight or change them? This doesn't mean that you must tolerate it further. To the contrary, once you accept that what's happening is just *happening*, you recognize that you can choose to exit of your own accord. You may choose to remove yourself — not because you were forced to leave, change, or move — but because you decided to take care of yourself and move to another state of being or a new physical position.

Often when we give up the fight or attempt to change things to suit our desires, things become clearer to us. Solutions seem to appear out of nowhere. You'll gain greater insight for problem solving when you stop assuming that things must change according to your plan. By simply allowing a situation *to be* without labeling it as wrong or bad, you free up your energy to move your life in a direction that's more aligned with your beliefs and values.

Besides situations, relationships, and circumstance, many people resist their emotions as well. This is a mistake we've all made, and it's one that holds us hostage the most.

See Your Emotions as Messengers

Emotion is simply energy in motion. After practicing integrative medicine and acupuncture for nearly two decades, I truly believe that emotions are messengers, too. We're not meant to stuff our emotions and feelings away or deny them the space to be. We are driven and motivated by our emotions, so paying attention to and consciously directing them can give us incredible power.

As you learned in the last chapter, one of the keys to self-compassion and mindfulness is to allow ourselves to see, feel, and be with our emotions without judgment. So, I invite you to open your mind and become the nonjudgmental witness to see emotions for what they are: messengers. Rather than forcing your emotions into the shadows, medicating them, or numbing them away with food, shopping, or drugs, bring them to the forefront of your attention to gently see the message they've come to communicate.

Practicing mindfulness offers you the opportunity to be present with your feelings and emotions in a nonjudgmental, non-shaming manner. This grants you a bit of safe distance to learn from the emotions and transmute their destructive energy into healing or productive energy, when possible. By becoming mindful of the energy in your emotions, you'll come to realize that you are not your emotions, and you need not be trapped by them. And you need not resist them either. Mindfulness invites you to stop collapsing your identity within the emotion. When you stop judging your emotions, you realize that having the so-called "negative" emotions of anger, fear, or sadness doesn't make you a bad person. You can allow them to bring you insight and move on.

In my clinical practice, I have noticed that when we block the flow of emotion and prevent their message from being received, the energy can be directed inward with destructive consequences. This can lead to physical pain, emotional distress, and even disease. When our emotional energy is blocked inside us and not expressed, we'll often see a blockage in other areas of our lives, presenting us with health challenges or emotional upsets that disrupt our relationships.

The antidote to blocking our emotions is to be present with them with an attitude of mindful acceptance and self-compassion.

As a nonjudgmental witness, you watch the emotions rise and disappear, without being trapped inside them. Studies show that mindfulness training can even prevent depression by encouraging individuals to accept and tolerate their painful thoughts and emotions rather than trying to change them, while simultaneously placing these thoughts and emotions in a larger context so their significance is seen with greater perspective.

Resistance is futile

Resisting your "negative" feelings and telling them to shut up or go away is like ignoring a tour guide who's standing by with a map and navigation directions pointing to the life of your dreams. Your feelings could be that helpful guide you brush off dismissively. You could foolishly continue bumbling along looking for a street that's behind you or in a completely different direction.

Instead of pushing feelings away, allow the situation and feelings to *be*. Stop yourself in your tracks and just watch life happening. Stop the mental labeling and observe. Allow your feelings and emotions to have a voice. You might ask yourself, "What am I resisting?" Or ask, "What am I grasping and clinging to?" Then wait for an answer to emerge. Your goal is ultimately to return to a flexible stance that allows you to be in flow.

So many of us hide our true feelings, especially the ones we consider negative or embarrassing. But what if instead of judging them as "bad" and banishing them to the nether regions of our minds, we allowed our emotions to be felt and expressed? What if we looked at every feeling as right instead of wrong? I'm not suggesting they be given permission to overtake your life, just that they be acknowledged and heard. So, ask yourself, "What is right and appropriate about this feeling, in this moment?"

Based on your aspiration or intention, when it comes time to start goal setting or planning your future, you should be in the most positive state possible. And certainly, if you're in problem-solving mode, having anxious or nervous energy bubbling within you could cause a major distraction. The key is to make sure that you're receptive to wisdom, insight, or healing by putting your mind, body, brain, and heart into a calm, open state. If you're in a negative state or resisting what's going on, it will be harder to experience peace or productivity.

Practice makes the master

Right now, imagine that you're in a challenged state of fear or anxiety where you just don't feel good. Remember a time when you felt stressed, overwhelmed, or unable to handle the pressures of life. How did your head feel in those situations? For me, it is in those times that I feel my head swimming or pounding like it could explode.

What about your stomach or the solar plexus area? What do you feel there? Is it butterflies in your stomach, a deep gnawing pain, or nausea?

What about your back and shoulders? When you're stressed, do you feel tension in the muscles in your neck and upper back?

What about your legs or feet? Do they feel restless and spastic when you're anxious?

The first step to getting into a more positive state is to first acknowledge and allow yourself to be in that state without resistance. You could try putting it into words, like this:

"I am really feeling anxious now. My thoughts are racing and I feel a twinge in my stomach. I feel so nervous like I'm juggling daggers and I'm about to drop them on my head. I feel like I can't deal with this! I feel tension between my shoulder blades and my muscles are tight and aching."

You know the expressions "getting something off your chest" or "get that monkey off your back"? This is when we feel weighed down, like we're carrying something heavy on our back and life feels like a burden. Or it's the sensation of something weighing so heavily on our chests and our hearts, that we almost can't breathe and we feel constricted. By expressing what you're feeling, you open up the possibility of releasing the negative tension in your body and energy field.

Once you're in touch with these tense feelings, it's a good time to breathe or sigh. To express what you're feeling without judgment can allow you to exhale tension as you give yourself permission, freedom, and space to be honest and vulnerable. And you really are breathing a sigh of relief as you get your emotions off your chest and mind. Many times, when you just say what you're experiencing, you feel a sense of lightness.

So, if you can, take a deep breath and say what you're feeling and let that be. You may feel the feelings rise up and by becoming the witness of them, you may notice that they just slightly separate from your body. That tension in your neck, the pang in your stomach will rise up and separate, as if it's hanging around your body like a puff of smoke.

Bringing your attention to what you're feeling allows you to see from the perspective of the Authentic Self, which is your consciousness — not your body. Take another deep breath and recognize that those feelings are there for a reason. Your emotions are energy in motion, bringing you a message. If you stuff them away and don't allow them to speak to you, they may go deeper and cause you pain, either now or later.

If you can allow the emotions to be there and give them a voice, you can take heart that you are on the first step toward freedom. The trick is to watch yourself if you stray into judging yourself or the feelings. For example, have you ever heard yourself say:

"Gosh, you face this problem every day! You should be able to deal with this by now!"

Or

"For heaven's sake, it's just email! You shouldn't be so overwhelmed by writing a few messages! Just crank them out and get it over with."

Or

"I'm so angry at myself! Why do I always do that?"

These mental assaults are filled with judgment that is counterproductive and self-defeating. If you can give yourself a break by letting the emotions bring you the lesson, you can move onto solutions.

Consider saying:

"Whoa! There I go judging myself again. It's kind of habit, huh?"

Then exhale.

ACCEPTANCE Opens The Door To TRANSCENDENCE

This small shift of perspective has allowed me to rid myself of decades of pain and guilt. I became an expert at stuffing my painful emotions down into the basement of my mind. I would simply force any remorse or upset away, usually with the thought that a healer or spiritual person *shouldn't* feel those negative emotions. Over time, I realized that those painful feelings were poised to drag me into a dark depression. As I allowed the shame and remorse I felt for past mistakes to bubble up to the surface of my mind, I faced them with tolerance and compassion. Then, almost miraculously, my heart began to feel lighter. Waves of relief and release move through body and mind when we stop denying painful emotions. That's when true healing begins and peace flourishes in our lives.

Frustration with parenting is another example I'm quite familiar with. I often work with mothers who are ashamed that they feel overwhelmed with parenting as they sheepishly admit to seriously disliking the mundane tasks of mommy-hood. I definitely felt this way when my daughter was little and still in diapers. Most clients are surprised when I tell them NOT to fight the thoughts or feelings of disgust. I encourage them to stop labeling the feelings as "bad." They fear that admitting to feeling burdened by parenting or not liking certain aspects of care-taking will make them a "bad parent."

Please know that the more you fight these thoughts, the more you make yourself out to be a bad person for thinking them in the first place. Internally you label yourself as bad, imperfect and wrong for thinking thoughts and having feelings you "shouldn't" have. You end up labeling yourself when you harshly judge the thoughts and feelings that you're so strongly attached to. This sort of self-criticism and self-judgment only leads to inner turmoil and unrest.

Finding displeasure in cleaning up the kitchen for the fifth time in a day, for example, doesn't mean you're a bad parent. It doesn't mean you love your children or spouse any less. We often give hidden meanings to these types of feelings, which stresses us out even more. We drive these feelings underground without any regard to the toll they take on us over time. Look at the feelings for the real message they bring, without judgment.

Emotions can be locked in the body

What are the consequences of trapped emotion? As explained earlier, all of our life experiences — from the ecstatic to the traumatic — form memories that are held in the body and mind. They get locked into our aura. When emotions are not allowed to flow freely, they don't get released for processing or recycling and the energy they carry can get lodged in our tissues, organs, muscles, etc. Toxic emotions can therefore have toxic effects on the cells of our body, destroying them, increasing chances of cancer, and accelerating the aging process.

By stuffing the emotions away with food or alcohol we perpetuate their ill effects. But like a small child wanting her mommy's attention, emotions will simply continue screaming and nagging until they're heard and given what they desire — which in most cases, is just loving attention.

Emotions exist on a spectrum

Each emotion literally has its own frequency it emits to the universe. While speaking with Yvette Taylor of EAM, she shared with me her understanding of how each of our emotions has its own energetic vibration. Take a look at the Energy Emotion Scale below. This chart was originally created by Dr. David Hawkins, author of *Power vs. Force*.

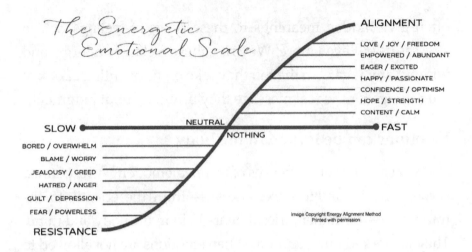

The Energetic Emotional Scale

ALIGNMENT

— LOVE / JOY / FREEDOM
— EMPOWERED / ABUNDANT
— EAGER / EXCITED
— HAPPY / PASSIONATE
— CONFIDENCE / OPTIMISM
— HOPE / STRENGTH
— CONTENT / CALM

SLOW ● — NEUTRAL — ● FAST
NOTHING

BORED / OVERWHELM
BLAME / WORRY
JEALOUSY / GREED
HATRED / ANGER
GUILT / DEPRESSION
FEAR / POWERLESS

RESISTANCE

Image Copyright Energy Alignment Method
Printed with permission

Bearing in mind that the heart is 5,000 times more powerful than the brain, our emotions are more important in directing our experience of life than our thoughts. So emotional management is critical to living a peaceful, productive, and purposeful life.

When it comes to our emotions, there are three things to know. There is the vibration, the intensity, and the speed. These are not the same.

Your emotional vibration describes the quality of the emotion

Some emotions, which you can see at the bottom of the scale, are a low vibration. These are emotions such as feelings of fear and depression. We experience them very much in this way too. You know those days when you just want to hide under the duvet and not see or speak to anyone? We feel low and drained of vitality.

Then we have emotions that are a high vibration, these are feelings of love, freedom, and abundance. That is exactly how we experience them, too. When we're happy, we feel excited to be alive, we want to sing and dance. It feels like we've been plugged into a vital source of life energy.

Your emotions have an intensity

Each emotion also has a vibrational intensity. The intensity of fear, for example, is all consuming. In fact, it can be almost paralyzing, because it feels so intense.

Now think about the feeling of frustration; while it is not a "positive" emotion, it does feel better than fear. There is a comparative lightness to it. Likewise, the emotions of calm or contentment are just very mellow. There is not really much energy or intensity to them.

Take yourself to the top of the scale and think about the emotion of love. Again, this can be all-consuming from an energy perspective. When you are in that real love state, you can't really think clearly. It takes up the whole of your energy in this alive, awakening, excited state.

So, the emotions toward the top and bottom and top are more intense, in the middle they are less so.

Your emotions have speed

Our emotions also have speed or velocity. When you look at the chart, you'll see at each end are the words fast and slow. The further toward the bottom and the left of the chart you go, the slower the emotion is. The closer to the top and the right you look, the faster the energy of the emotion is.

Now when we think about speed, we're talking about the speed at which you create or change things. We consider how quickly things will change when you're in that emotion. When you're in each of these emotional states, it's affecting your ability to create change in your life. So, if you want things to change and you want to enjoy more of your life experience, your work is to maintain these positive emotions (that is anything above the line, or the neutral point). This means when we are spending time in feelings of calm, contentment, happiness, passion, love, and joy, we are working *with the universe.*

If you're spending your time over on the other side, in feelings of irritation and frustration, you cannot manifest from this space. In that case, things feel like a struggle and don't seem to change quickly.

So, you will learn how to release the stuck or resistant emotions (and the thoughts or situations that are creating them) using the Energy Alignment Method described in the next section. With EAM, you can align your energy to the new positive emotions you want to experience.

Summary of practical tips for becoming peaceful in the ALLOW phase

When driven by negativity, shift into Neutral

Relinquish the need to control what is happening, including your feelings. There's no need to resist your feelings or emotions. Our feelings are messengers and our emotions are "energy in motion." Allow the charge of these energetic messengers to be transformed into a neutral charge and a positive state will soon follow.

Discharge tension — cry, scream, shake, exercise

For the rest of the day (or all week long, if you dare!) resist the temptation to judge your feelings for yourself. Allow them to just be, and let yourself fully experience them. . Move yourself to a safe place and cry, scream, shake or do whatever you need to in order to discharge some of the negative energy without harming yourself or others.

Describe the emotion

Breathe deeply and allow the emotion to just be there. Allow yourself to feel what you feel. Name the feeling or emotion.

Out loud you could say, "Right now I am feeling _____ (ex: anger, frustration, sadness)." Allow yourself to freely express exactly what you're feeling without censoring yourself. For example, you might say "Wow, I am feeling really angry and pissed off! Being around that person made my blood boil."

Your feelings are not you, so there is no reason to become defensive just because you feel an unpleasant emotion. As much as you consider yourself spiritual or evolved, you're also human. The ego is alive and has a long-held habit of reacting.

Find the feeling in the body

Can you locate the feelings in your body? Try to notice where in your body your emotions lie. Then describe the feeling out loud. For example, you may say, "I feel tension in my neck and now my stomach is doing flips!"

Ask for insight

Ask yourself what message that emotion is bringing to you. Is it insecurity, fear, embarrassment? Next, go directly to the source of your discomfort and ask the feeling, "What message do you have for me?" Asking what it wants or what the lesson is may help you see yourself with more compassion and understanding.

You may not hear the response from your body or mind right away. Just know that the truth is ever present, and when your heart and mind are open, the wisdom will come to you.

There's no need to censor the answers that come to you either. Often, when we ask ourselves why we are angry, for example, we get self-entitled snotty comments in return. "Well duh! I'm angry because my boss is an idiot who can't explain projects properly and expects the world to respond to his every whim!"

Or, "Obviously I'm ticked off because my spouse simply doesn't do his/her fair share around the house! What am I, a maid?"

Allow the feelings to bring the messages — the thoughts or beliefs — that are holding them up. Often when you really get down to the underlying message you realize that it, too, may be upheld by beliefs or biases that YOU can change, if necessary.

For example, imagine you've asked yourself "Why am I feeling so upset at my kid for cheating on his math test?" Your first response may seem obvious: "I'm mad because cheating is wrong. He could get expelled!" But when you dig deeper perhaps there's yet another thought underlying the angry feeling. Something like, "His cheating reminds me of when I was caught looking at someone's paper in school and my father called me stupid." In this example, projecting a strong fear of humiliation or condemnation is what really underlies the upset.

By just **allowing** the message to come up you can look at the situation again, with slightly less toxic energy. **NOTE:** At this stage you are still not trying to go into problem solving mode. This step is just about allowing the emotions and feelings to be seen, heard, felt, and named. Your goal here is to ease the tension and get to neutral. It's rarely effective or productive to problem solve when you're in a low energy state.

In later stages of the Attunement Meditation™, when you're really aligned with a higher state of consciousness and vibrating to the rhythm of love and compassion, you'll find that solutions become clear. You'll find it becomes easy and gentle to let go of hurts, prejudices, and painful emotions.

Release the toxic emotions with a clearing statement

The Energy Alignment Method (EAM) includes a 5-step process for releasing stuck emotions and energy. For more insights, get a copy of *The Ultimate Self-Help Book: How to Be Happy Confident & Stress Free, Change Your Life with Law Of Attraction & Energy Healing.*

The EAM process includes an energy a release statement that allows you to transform and discharge toxic emotions. Once you've gotten in touch with the emotion, located it in the body, and even heard the message it has to bring, you can repeat the release statement to return to a neutral energy state. Repeat this statement at least three times or until you can no longer feel it. (You may have to do this another two or three times.)

"I am ready to release _____ (whatever the emotion).

I release it from my energy in all forms, on all levels and at all points in time."

Other examples:

"I am ready to release this hard, red ball in my stomach when I think about work.

I release this anxiety from my energy in all forms, on all levels, at all points in time."

"I am ready to release this image of a brick wall in front of me.

I release it from my energy in all forms, on all levels, at all points in time."

Visit www.EnergyAlignmentMethod.com to see videos of Yvette explaining how to apply the release statement to a variety of emotions and situations, and to learn the entire 5-step process.

Feeling too overwhelmed? Walk away!

If you find yourself in the midst of a tense situation and you can't clear your head enough to hear anything other than negativity, you'll need to get yourself into a neutral or positive energy state *before* trying to allow and accept things as they are. When you're feeling threatened or angry the primitive parts of your brain are active and the "survival" solutions that come to you will often be selfish or destructive.

If you're feeling unstable, supercharged, or hostile, walk away — renew your positive energy. During this time try to avoid replaying the events in your mind. Re-living negative experiences creates a trigger for more stress hormones and contributes to a depressed mood, weakened immune system, and clouded judgment. Stabilize the situation if it's critical, then walk away and do something you enjoy that will renew your energy. Or try to distract yourself with exercise, housework, or by listening to music.

When under pressure or stress, men are generally great at moving into another energy state by engaging in physical activity while women tend to stew in their emotional upsets, drowning in negativity. If you feel that you're too distressed to even think straight, I find that meridian tapping processes like Thought Field Therapy and the Emotional Freedom technique work wonders. These techniques, described briefly here, are helpful for bringing calm to the body and mind and are quite useful in helping us get into a more resourceful and peaceful state.

Thought Field Therapy

Thought Field Therapy (TFT) is the body tapping procedure discovered by Dr. Roger Callahan over thirty years ago to alleviate phobias, anxiety, and stress. With TFT you "tap" on specific points on the body in a sequence along the same energy meridians that acupuncture follows. This sort of self-acu-tapping helps to balance the body's energy system. The specific tapping sequences are considered healing codes, which allow you to eliminate most negative emotions within minutes while promoting the body's own healing ability.

TFT is a unique form of meridian therapy that is a natural, drug-free, needle-free system to eliminate the cause of negative emotions. TFT has been shown to be extraordinarily effective in treating several psychological problems.

TFT also includes a diagnostic process where a practitioner helps to determine the cause of the emotional upset to prescribe the appropriate tapping algorithm. Sometimes muscle testing, or kinesiology is used here. You can learn more about TFT in a beautiful book called *The Book on Quantum Leaps for Leaders* written by my friend and colleague, Bitta Wiese. She has successfully used this modality to heal herself of debilitating pain after a parachute accident and later to rebuild her self-esteem.

Bitta explains how TFT was first used with spoken affirmations to treat and reverse severe traumatic reactions. TFT has since been used for weight loss and to stop smoking, and in overcoming painful losses, phobias, physical ailments, sexual trauma, and much more.

The reason it works is because when we think of a particular problem (such as a specific fear), we generate an individual thought field in much the same way as an electrical field is generated around electrical equipment. According to Dr. Callahan's theory, emotional problems are generated by specific interference patterns in these thought fields, which he describes as "perturbations." These perturbations have been found to be the generating power behind the emotional (and occasionally, physical) signs and symptoms recognized by conventional medicine.

Most existing therapies simply attempt to subdue those symptoms with varying degrees of success, or teach the patient coping skills. Whatever the outcome of such treatments, the perturbations in the Thought Field (the cause of the problem in the first place) remain. In order to remove the perturbations completely, and therefore the problem itself, one must apply a code that nature has provided. Dr. Callahan outlined several specific tapping sequences to treat emotional conditions and he believes that tapping in sequence does make a big difference.

Dr. Callahan found that some people believed it was the affirmation that helped and not the tapping, or some resisted the therapy because the affirmation seemed too simple. So, after proving that TFT tapping sequences could be equally effective without the affirmation, he eliminated them from the standard protocol that's taught today.

The difference between TFT and EFT

An American named Gary Craig studied TFT with Dr. Callahan and began using it with clients in the United States. He found that one tapping algorithm or "basic recipe" could replace the multitude of algorithms for specific conditions, which he now affirms works in over 80% of cases. That basic recipe, derived from TFT algorithms, is what is now known as EFT — the Emotional Freedom Technique. EFT also eliminates the broad use of muscle testing that often accompanies TFT diagnosis.

The combination of tapping the energy meridians and voicing positive affirmations works to clear the "short-circuit" — the emotional block — from your body's bioenergy system, thus restoring your mind and body's balance, which is essential for optimal health and the healing of physical disease.

You can use TFT or EFT to discharge the tension and negativity you feel and to break the neurological connections between the negative thoughts and emotions. I've found both are great ways to allow the stressful emotions to be there while you access a better energy state.

You can see an interview I did with Bitta where she outlines the basic TFT protocol. You can also download a couple of chapters of her book by visiting www.RealSelf.love

Imagine The Alternative

Before moving to the next part of The Attunement Meditation, consider these final questions: can you let life FLOW without attachment to any predefined outcomes? Even your dreams and desires, can they flow into view and be released without feeling a needy sense of lack? How high could life take you if you were free from heavy thoughts, compulsions, and *shoulds*? To what heights of joy, ecstasy and LOVE could you soar if you let the wind carry you where it may?

Remember:

- feelings are messengers
- resistance is futile
- be open to consider that every feeling may be "right"
- be mindful to not lock your emotions in your body

- your first step toward peace is also to shift into a neutral emotional state

Consider doing the following as you let intense emotional energies rise and fall away.

- describe the emotion

- find the feeling in the body

- ask for insight on what the emotion wants to tell you

- use the Energy Alignment Method's release statement

- walk away

- consider doing meridian tapping therapy (EFT / TFT)

- pray

- meditate

- surrender

- cease fighting your disease, sickness, or circumstance

Once you've achieved a neutral energy state by allowing the energy and emotions to come to the surface to be acknowledged, heard, understood, and released, it's time to move into a positive energy state. We move up the emotional scale from neutral to positive with the next part of the Attunement Meditation: ATTUNE.

Attune

Have you ever been in love? Have you ever felt inspired by the love you feel toward a child, a treasured pet, or a beautiful place? If so then you may have noticed that when you're feeling positive emotions of appreciation, admiration, and love, your life just seems to flow smoothly and your response to stressful situations is nothing short of miraculous. When we are filled with love, it's easier to let little things slide off our backs without much rancor or negativity.

While living in the love zone we don't need as much sleep, food, or private time. Love provides an amazing inspiration; a passionate creative life energy that makes nearly everything exciting, happy, and bright. Love can make unpleasant things bearable. Sometimes when we're in love we have great insights and inspiration, and we sense that there's a divine force that illuminates us.

In this step we Attune ourselves and come into resonance with the frequency of love.

In the previous section we learned that the first step is to mindfully **Allow** the emotions and situations of the present moment the right to exist without judgment. This helps to create space in our mind for new possibilities to emerge. That spaciousness also allows for a quiet acceptance of what is happening. You may still desire that things were in a different state, but after deep breathing, praying, meditating, meridian tapping, listening to music, exercising, or whatever you did to allow it to be, you may notice that there is more peace and spaciousness. You create more space for solutions to appear or come to mind.

It's difficult to make leaps up the emotional scale. But from a peaceful place of neutrality, you can tap into the energetic field of positivity and infinite possibility. You can move from neutral to positive by bringing your heart into resonance with love or compassion. That's how you'll access a vibrational state of resiliency, power, and creativity. Your ability to transform your situation or transcend the negativity will then be amplified. Some would say that a perfect resolution to your situation can only come from the field of love and compassion.

"The solution to problems will never be found at the level of the problem. The solution will always come from love."

~ Deepak Chopra

When you first Attune, you'll connect with your heart energetically, and literally feel it beating in your chest. Then you'll connect your heart to the energetic presence of love all around you. You will then project loving energy out to the rest of the world.

Begin by closing your eyes and breathing deeply for a few breaths. Place your hand on your chest and feel your heart beating. Taking five long, slow deep breaths will allow you to bring down your blood pressure and heart rate, and will help to lower stress hormones. If you close your eyes and feel your heart, you'll find that it starts to beat with more regularity and calmness. As you synchronize your breathing and heart rate to a frequency of the Earth, you get out of fight-flight-freeze mode. You become tuned into the peaceful frequency that the Mother Gaia emits. Lowering the stress response with deep breathing and feeling your heart tells the reptilian brain, "Hey, this is not life or death! You can chill out. There's no tiger about to eat us!"

Continue with your eyes closed and breathing deeply. Imagine that you are tuned into the "radio station of love, peace, and harmony." What thoughts or words would you hear on that radio station? Imagine the radio waves seeping into your body and mind to melt away tension and stress. What would that feel like in your body? Feel your body relax into a wave of peace and love. Imagine that you're surrounded by a warm caress of loving energy.

By tuning into love, we put ourselves into a more resourceful state. When connected with the field of love, you gain admission to the world of possibility, pure potential, and peace.

Love grants us access to a state associated with our own best outcome and the highest good of all the people tied to the issue. It helps us to put the m'ego on hold, the part of us that is preoccupied with survival of "me." By tuning into love, you tap into the divine consciousness that is associated with the survival of *everyone*. There are no winners, no losers. There may be compromise, but it's all done in the spirit of love.

Next, look around for anything that inspires love. Perhaps consider why you're on this planet and what's worth living for. What motivates you? Or you may imagine the sweet face of a child, a little kitten, or remember a time when you felt inspired by love in nature such as by a beautiful sunset, a beach vacation, or hiking in the mountains. If you can see any of those things around you while doing the deep breathing, go ahead and observe them. If not, close your eyes and put yourself back in one of those scenes.

Try to imagine that there is a force field of love surrounding you. Get the sense of gentle waves of love coming from the radio station of love and harmony. Those waves are always present in the air. Just like the waves of every radio station in your city are waiting to be accessed by your radio antenna, so too are the waves of love. Your radio will play music from the station to which you tune your receiver. You are a human antenna and you can also choose which frequency to receive. By just becoming quiet, going within, breathing, and focusing on anything that inspires love, gratitude, and compassion you can access the accompanying frequency. In the vibrational frequency of love is inspiration, higher wisdom, possibility, and potentiality.

Continue to breathe slowly and deeply. Focus on anything that you can love or appreciate. If you can say "I love you" to yourself, do that.

This is a good time to recite the phrases of the loving kindness meditation we learned in Chapter 4. Bring to mind someone who loves you dearly. Imagine them standing next to you, sending you positive waves of love and compassion. You can also imagine sending yourself sincere wishes to be free from suffering. Or imagine yourself as a small, innocent child and send this image of loving energy.

The Energy Alignment Method offers a positive affirmation statement to help you welcome in positive vibes. You should repeat this statement at least three times or until you feel it in your energy.

"I am ready to receive / create / feel / manifest / experience
_____" (whatever the subject).

I allow this into my energy, in all forms, on all levels, at all points in time."

As you allow yourself to bask in this positive wave of energy, you'll gradually build up energy reserves that help you to become more resilient, more resourceful, and less reactive. This is an important part of becoming the best version of yourself, no matter what craziness is happening in the world around you.

From this state of positive energy and emotion, you can now move to the next stage, ALIGN.

Align

Now you'll align your mind with higher states of consciousness. What does that mean? Well, normally in the beginning phases of the process, when we're stressed out or we're trying to solve a problem, our focus is very limited or narrow. Typically, the brain only has access to what's already been programmed. When we're stressed or threatened, the brain becomes intensely focused on your own survival, and that of the things or people you hold dear.

When you want to chart a new course in life, write a new book, or solve a problem, you want to be a little more open to greater possibilities and greater wisdom, right? It will be worthwhile to align your mind with a higher mind, one tuned into greater wisdom and insight. This higher mind could be your higher self, the part of you that is divine or enlightened. Or you might want to tune into the Holy Spirit, or God, or whatever higher state of being you think might be guiding you and supporting you. It may be that, just as Einstein and so many other physicists have talked about, we can tap into the higher capabilities of our own natural brain.

So how do we do that on a practical level?

The first thing to do is to give yourself permission and instruction to do so. In step one, we quieted down the chaos, and we allowed ourselves to come to neutral. In step two, we attuned to positivity. Being in a calmer state creates new connections between the lower brain and the higher brain that we don't have when we're stressed. When we're attuned to love, we are much more open to new ways of thinking and new ways of seeing problems.

You're already learning how to *really* tune into your body. Consider what happens to you when you come up against someone you may have had a problem with, or that you know has strong opinions. Does your body or mind get full of tension, like mine can? Many of us tend to close down; we tend to become either defensive or offensive, to maintain our position.

Consider what would happen if you felt that tension and said, "oh, okay, I see where this is going, you're feeling threatened." Then take those deep breaths, which are saying to the brain "hey, I'm aware here, this is not a tiger, this is not a big bear, I can handle this. My life is not in danger." This opens us up to positivity where we could consider how to help this person live with ease so that we all get what we need in this situation.

Step three of the process invites you to align with the mind of the Divine where you might say, "Not my will, but Thy will be done." Aligning your mind with the mind of Love, which desires the best outcome for ALL people involved, takes you out of ego-based desires. You can choose to line up your thoughts, will, and desires with a state of higher consciousness. The Mind of the Divine has the answers to all problems anyway. So, you really can't go wrong!

When I say align your mind with the higher mind, or divine mind, you're literally going to say to yourself, "may my mind be guided by peace and love." Or, "may my mind be open to new wisdom." So, as you're sitting at home, in your car, or standing in line, after you've brought that calm to yourself and tapped into love, you can let go of your own ideas about how things should shift by saying, "may my mind be guided by higher wisdom." It's that simple.

You are making a conscious decision to open your mind to other possibilities, rather than being fixed on the ego's insistence on "my way, my way, my way." Normally, when we go into problem solving, we have an opinion of what we think is best. For example, when we're negotiating or fighting with someone, we want to win, we want our point to get across. Sometimes, we might actually be right and our way may lead to greater success. But there comes a point in life when you want harmony, and when you desire peace rather than being right. Yes, you still want the best resolution, but you want the best resolution for everyone involved. In life, we don't always need to think of being the winner while others are the losers.

When you align your mind to the higher mind, aligning it to these higher states of consciousness, you're allowing an opening. It's about opening up and letting go of your agenda and your perspective, to maybe be more compassionate and to see things from another person's point of view. It may be that who you're dealing with at the moment thinks that they're right; they may really want to get their way. You might choose to give them their way, but you want to be informed by the highest wisdom possible.

When we align, there's not much to do other than to just be quiet, present, and open. All that you've heard in the first lessons about mindfulness, about letting go of these rigid attachments, and becoming more open to what is here — this is one of those keys, when we are just *open*. We don't have to judge, and we don't have to criticize or label. You just need to decide. We create the intention to be led by higher wisdom.

You could also imagine yourself performing and interacting at your best in the current situation and align yourself in this moment with the thinking and attitude of your Best You. What does your highest state of mind tell you about who you really are in this situation? Align with the mental concept, mannerisms, and beliefs of your Best You, to the best of your ability now. What is the least you can align with now? What is the most you could accept as truth right now?

Make a decision to line up your thoughts, feelings, and actions with your Best You, your higher Self, the God in you.

Most people tell me that when they really decide that they're going to be open to higher wisdom, they start to see tons of synchronicities in their lives where the people they were thinking about suddenly call them on the phone and they wonder, "how did you know?" Or they get an email, or some problem resolves itself when they let go of that rigid control.

I want you to do an experiment. As you get into really opening yourself up to higher wisdom, or creativity, or intuition, I want you to just keep track of all the times that you find the little confirmations in your life where insight comes in. What might change in your life? Well, we never know, but once you have that openness, and that awareness to tune in and look for it, you might find that there is always this sort of hand guiding you and leading you in life. When we can be more open and accepting of it, we really get blessed with these gifts of intuition, insight, and creativity. So, your assignment, if you choose to accept it, is to just go into situations and bring a more open perspective.

Act on Inspiration

Acting on inspiration is all about taking that open mind that we just developed and going a little bit further into openness. You will either take action when you've been truly inspired, or you wait and do *nothing*. You *literally* wait for inspiration. Now, of course if you're dealing with a major crisis, you can't always just sit back and say, "I'm waiting on inspiration." But in most situations in our life, if we stabilize what's going on, and go away either for a few minutes or a few hours to bring back a sense of calm, to connect again with love, to align with higher wisdom, and to open our mind and heart, we can say to ourselves: "okay, I'm only going to take action on inspiration."

This is the principle behind the popular practice of 'sleeping on it' before making a major decision.

Knowing that your thoughts and intentions determine your entire life experience — mentally and physically — you'll find the action that is inspired by Love, your higher self or soul, that is in line with your highest ideals and values, is the only action worth taking. This is the ultimate in taking responsibility for our choices, thoughts, and emotions.

Inspiration, in Latin is *in-spiritus;* it means you're connected with the spiritual side of life. And as I've said, the spirit in you really does want the best for you and everyone. Spiritual wisdom is generally connected to everything in the universe, so I tend to think that it knows better than my limited thinking mind.

I like to say that armed with true self-awareness, self-acceptance, and accountability, the "right" path becomes obviously clear. You will come to see, feel, or otherwise sense which actions are beneficial for your life expression, and are in line with your values, and which are aligned with Love. You may find that circumstances spontaneously appear and you know the best course for you. Or, as you embark on a path, you become sensitive to the need to stop, wait, or leave a situation all together.

While exploring this stage, you'll learn to achieve a receptive state to receive guidance and inspiration to create a personal plan of action leading you toward goals you believe are appropriate for you now. All the while, you learn to allow for the unexpected insights that will come when you get really tuned into living life according to your own destiny. Acting on inspiration prepares you for a new way of life that promises more peace, harmony, and fulfillment, which positions you to fully enjoy life!

You are freed from doing busy work that doesn't please you, or mindless activities that fail to advance you on your soul's journey. Instead, you begin to live with intention and purpose. You are encouraged to tap into your own internal wisdom and guidance from your higher self, the Soul or what you may call intuition. This means that you don't have to feel like you're just trying to solve problems, batting against something that's just not working, or filling up your schedule because you have to *look* busy. It allows you this space and the consciousness and the heart resonance to say, "I'm now choosing to live my life in a different way. I'm going to live my life in accordance with my highest values." So, when you feel inspired to take action, *that's* when you'll take action.

It can feel a little risky because most of us are programmed to act fast, to be proactive, and all of which is very good, especially for us entrepreneurs. But when you want to get to a point where you are living on a higher plane of existence, you must tune into the creativity, inspiration, insight, and the spiritual presence that really governs all of life. In this way, the decisions that you make are the right ones for you, not just for right *now*, but for the long run. This part of the process is all about asking for inspiration, and not taking action until you have it.

Intuition vs Rational Thinking

So how do you know when it's truly intuition or higher wisdom, and not just your rational mind? Well, this also takes practice. So once again, at the end of the day or at the end of the week, I want you to write down, all the times when you had a hunch, or a *feeling* that you should or shouldn't have done something, and then write about the result.

Take note of the insight and inspiration your intuition brings you. One way to do this is to look over the last year and think about all the significant milestones and any major decisions that you had to make, as well as any major catastrophes that you had to deal with. Then go back to those decision points, and look at the period just before. Before that decision, were there any feelings that you had about what you should or shouldn't do? Was there a hunch or voice in your head saying "Hmm... watch out"?

If you go back over the last year or several years and look at the major turning points in your life — the major decisions you made about your work, your relationships, moving to a different place — what were those feelings, what were those thoughts, what were the things that you heard in your mind? Or what were the things you saw in your environment that you felt were really trying to lead you in a certain direction? Write those down.

You can also write about what you did or *didn't* do based on those feelings. So many of us have a feeling like "oooh... I know I shouldn't eat that" or "something's telling me I just shouldn't go to this event." But we drag ourselves out, we let our rational mind talk us into things based on a promise we made. Or we may worry that it might look bad if we don't follow through, or whatever. In other words, we rationalize.

How many times have you gone ahead and done that thing and then regretted it? I want you to be able to see if there are patterns in your life that you can tune into.

Becoming aware of how you already have your natural genius abilities inside of you, that you are naturally guided, you are naturally tapped into universal wisdom, is the first step to becoming more sensitive to it and trusting it.

The best way to trust your intuition, is to make a list of all the times it comes up, what decisions you do and don't make, and what the outcomes are. Looking back, you might say, "wow, I could've trusted myself in that situation" or "I knew that was the way I was supposed to go. I should have listened to myself." Then you can start being proactive and as you move forward you can ask yourself at any major decision point, "how am I feeling, what's my body telling me? What's my mind telling me? Are there any little messages coming up through my dreams, or through my conversations, or things going on in my environment?"

The more you are willing to give yourself a moment of open awareness, the more you'll find that that wisdom continues to flow in, and that's when you'll know you are acting on *true inspiration* and not just your *rational mind*, so make a list. I'd love to hear about the really, really, juicy ones, where you just *knew* you shouldn't be in that relationship, or you just *knew* you shouldn't take that job, or you just *knew* you should've gone on that trip and you heard later how everyone had an amazing time.

Appreciate Life

The fifth and final part of the Attunement Meditation is Appreciation. Here we take a moment to *really* look at anything in our life, anything in our immediate surroundings, or in our world that we can appreciate. Then we consciously generate a feeling of gratitude for it. This part is about taking positivity to the next level and radiating it forward and outward through everything that we do. (You'll have lots of practice with this one as Appreciation is also the last step of the Cornerstone Process.)

Barbara Fredrickson, who's done extensive research on her "broaden and build theory" says that practicing positive emotions, like gratitude, can help broaden our repertoire of problem-solving abilities. The experience of positive emotions can protect us and actually help us rebound after stressful situations. We can even build up positivity, which helps us become more resourceful when life gets challenging. So, by proactively tuning into love, opening our mind and our heart to higher wisdom, and then generating these feelings of gratitude and appreciation, we're putting positivity coins in the bank.

Did you start a gratitude journal as I suggested at the end of Chapter 3? I totally love them and highly recommend you start writing in one daily. I encourage my clients to get into a nightly practice of writing down three to five things they are grateful for. This causes us to be more mindful of what we can be truly grateful for, even the little things. We take for granted so much in life without noticing the good, positive, lovely things that happen. Generating the feeling of gratitude can help us amplify positivity within our aura. And what we store in our aura will be sent out to the world around us, attracting things of a similar vibration into our field.

Beyond just writing what you're grateful for, the 3 Blessings exercise from Chapter 3 invites you to note the things that went right in your day and what role you played in them. When you can see that you actually played a part, even just as a witness or a non-active participant, you recognize that you have a place in the world that matters.

So, what are you grateful for? What relationships are you grateful for? Are you grateful for you being willing to read a book like this? Are you willing to appreciate the time that you've put into doing the daily rituals to send yourself compassion? Even these small things can add up.

Fredrickson's research has shown that allowing ourselves to appreciate these small wins can add up to much bigger rewards in terms of our physical and emotional health. This impacts how we interact with others and how we see the world. So, this step of the Attunement Meditation invites you to look around in your immediate environment or within your present circumstances to see what you can appreciate.

The Attunement Meditation initially came out of my need to help patients manage times where they were either stressed, dealing with an addiction, or dealing with crisis. Usually a person goes through the Attunement to bring calm to body and brain, to create more harmony in themselves and in others, so that when they move ahead they're inspired and take action that's for the highest amount of good.

Sometimes when we're in a situation where life is going nuts around us, it's hard to appreciate *anything*. It might be much easier to say, "man, my life sucks, everything's going wrong, this person's wrong, etc." We can literally create this spiral of negativity and look at everything that's going wrong in our lives. It's precisely during those times that we must remind ourselves that everything is temporary and nothing lasts forever. So, if you want to connect the dots between everything negative in your life, you could, but you know where that leads you right? It doesn't lead you where you want to go. So why not look for everything positive that you can, whether you're in a stressed situation or you're in a happy one.

Proactively build up positive resources within you. So, even in the midst of anger, irritability, frustration, or an addictive craving, once you bring that calm to body and brain and mind and heart, look around for something, *anything*, that can be appreciated. Is the sun shining? Then just take that in, notice it and appreciate it.

The wonderful work of Rick Hanson who wrote *Buddha's Brain* and *Hardwiring Happiness* involves a process that he calls "taking in the good." The basic concept is this: we literally need to spend five, ten, fifteen or up to thirty seconds to really absorb and appreciate the good things that are going on in our lives.

We have to do this for a half a minute sometimes, because, as he puts it, the mind is sort of like Velcro for bad or negative experiences. They stick to our minds and we get focused on them. Unfortunately, when it comes to positive experiences, our minds are more like Teflon. They don't tend to stick without some effort on our part.

So rather than letting the good stuff enter your mind while barely taking notice or letting it pass away quickly, I want you to actively take note of what you can appreciate in this world. Then savor it and let it soak in so that you remain in that positive frame of mind and being.

If everything is going crazy in my world, and I'm following this guideline, I'm going to look at what's positive to appreciate around me. I see that the sun is shining, I may even say out loud, "isn't it beautiful the way the sun glistens on those leaves and contrasts the light and the shadows," really taking it in and appreciating it.

Many people find it hard to appreciate anything when they're really sick. This is when you have to look at what might be considered mundane things. Maybe it's the texture of the cushion you're sitting on, or maybe it's the warmth or softness of the blanket that's around you. Perhaps it's just the cup of tea you're sipping, which warms you. The point is to be present to what you can appreciate, what you can be grateful for, and allow it to soak in.

So literally spending a few seconds to feel that sense of gratitude and appreciation is the key. The reason it's helpful to write it down, is because you're getting the emotion to settle into your body. You're actually allowing yourself to see it, feel it, write it, remember it, and cherish it. And that impacts your brain and your energy field, your aura.

If you don't already have a gratitude journal where you list the things in your life that you're grateful for, or the three blessings of the day, then I suggest that you get one. Of course, with technology, there are some really cool smartphone apps out there that will ask you "what are you grateful for today?" and you can type them in.

When life is going crazy and you're feeling bad, you can pick up your gratitude journal and go back and read through the entries that remind you that there is good in your life, you've done good things, you've made great progress, and there are things worth being grateful and happy about. When you meditate on happiness and the sense of gratitude, it makes you more open and willing to engage in life rather than shutting down and isolating yourself. For most of us, what happens when we go within is that we tend to look to the *past* and we see all the things we've done wrong and all the programming that led us to a certain point. Instead, mindfulness and meditation is calling us to be in this *present* moment with a lot more openness, curiosity, and awareness, so that we can see what's new, see where our life can take us *now,* and see what good we can bring out of ourselves in this moment.

If you're finding it difficult to get to the elevated feeling of appreciation, it may help to work your way up the emotional scale by deliberately experiencing joy, amusement and humor, which have been proven to help us build resources to deal with life's many challenges and negative emotional experiences.

My daughter and I enjoy watching inspiring TED talks to remind ourselves that our problems are really small and that there are many ways to overcome the blues. Others enjoy watching videos of baby animals doing funny or heroic things to bring a sense of wonder and awe back to their day.

Also, watching comedy films or reading a joke a day allows laughter to increase your mood and your happy hormones, like serotonin, dopamine and oxytocin.

Hugging someone for at least 10 seconds can also provide a feeling of comfort, safety and connection plus it gives a brain boost of oxytocin to help you stay upbeat. Plus playing or singing music and dancing boosts my feel-good chemicals almost instantly.

Another of my favorites mood boosters comes from wearing a SMILER, a magical instrument of joy created by a beautiful Icelandic artist and author named Gegga Birgis.

"If you smile five times per day for NO REASON, you can change your life in 90 days."

This quote by the Vietnamese monk, Thich Nhat Hanh, inspired Gegga to create a little helper that when put into your mouth makes you smile. In an inspiring video of one of her speeches online, Gegga shared how she used laughter and gratitude to heal from a dramatic facial injury. It's worth checking out, visit www.Smiler.is

So, there you have it. The last step of the Attunement Meditation invites you to look around and appreciate and be grateful for what is working in your life. Your daily assignment is to write down either the three blessings of the day, three things that went right and the part that you played in them, even if it's just as an observer of those three good things, or to write down things that you appreciate or you're grateful for. It could be people, it could be activities, or it could be this book. You could be grateful for yourself, appreciating that you've been such a trooper in your life that you keep going and don't give up. Write those things down and make sure that you savor them and let that good stuff sink in.

Living with Appreciation and gratitude is also the last step of the Cornerstone Process, which you'll see ends the book with a similar invitation to focus on gratitude.

Download a free guided meditation audio of the Attunement Meditation at www.RealSelf.love.

The Attunement Meditation™

ALLOW: Take 5 deep breaths and allow yourself to settle into a quiet state of awareness. Allow your thoughts to come up without resistance. Allow yourself to tune into the feelings, emotions and physical sensations, again, without resistance. Become the witness to the thoughts, feelings, and sensations. Allow their messages to come into your awareness without judgment.

ATTUNE: Imagine you have a loving or compassionate being sending out positive vibes your way. There is always love around us, the energy of nurturing, kindness and compassion. Imagine this positive energy swirling around you and draw it into you through your breath and intention. Know that you are cared for.

ALIGN: In a gentle act of surrender, mentally decide to align your mind with the highest thoughts possible. Open your mind to receive the wisdom of the Divine Mind. Say, 'may my mind be guided by peace, love and higher wisdom.

INSPIRED ACTION: Ask for guidance from your higher self, Source or God for the next inspired step you should take in your life. Listen, stay open, and expect an answer now or in the near future.

APPRECIATION: Find something in your environment or a memory in your heart to appreciate. Focus on one thing of beauty or anything good, lovely, positive, joyful, funny thing to appreciate. Carry this positive vibe with you.

The Cornerstone Process
Step 4 — Inspired Action

Can I be true to myself and take action? How will my transformation unfold?

As we take responsibility for our lives we move on to the fourth step in the Cornerstone Process, which introduces the opportunity for Inspired Action. In Step 4 you'll explore the processes that ensure that you **allow** your transformation to unfold with **inspired action** while remaining open to change. Focused on a positive emotion-filled productive future, you'll create your own personalized plan. Your plan will take into account potential pitfalls to avoid and actions to take in times of distress to prevent setbacks on your journey to a life of purpose and joy. And you'll learn to remain detached from the outcome so you flow through life with more ease and grace.

Knowing that your thoughts and intentions determine your entire life experience — mentally and physically — you'll find the action that is inspired by your spirit, which is in line with your highest ideals and values, is the only action worth taking. You'll be freed from doing busy work or activities that don't please you or advance you on your life journey.

In this step you are encouraged to tap into your internal wisdom, guidance from your higher self, your spirit or what you may call intuition. You'll come to see, feel, or otherwise sense, which actions are beneficial for your life expression and which are in line with your values. Armed with true self-awareness, self-acceptance, and accountability, the path to take becomes obviously clear. You may find that circumstances spontaneously appear and you know the right course for you. Or, as you embark on a path of action, you become sensitive to the need to stop, wait, or leave a situation all together.

While exploring the fourth step you'll learn to get into a receptive state to receive guidance and inspiration to manifest whatever you want in life. You will also learn to **allow** for the unexpected insights that will come when you get really tuned into living life according to your own destiny. A personalized plan of action to follow toward goals you believe are right for you now comes next. Step 4 will prepare you for a new way of life that promises more peace, harmony, and fulfillment. Then you'll be poised to enjoy creating and living your epic life!

To begin, first think about what would inspire you to get up in the morning. What is it that gives or would give your life meaning? Do you feel a sense of purpose in what you are doing?

Having a purpose to live for, or what the Japanese call "Ikigai" has been clinically shown to correlate with greater life satisfaction and a longer, disease-free life. Part of the reason purpose is helpful is that it causes changes in the brain that allow us to adapt to stress and puts us in a state of optimism and hope.

When you choose to use your strengths and talents in service to others you can increase your sense of meaning. Choosing to include service, charity and contributing to others is one of the most life-affirming practices to give your life meaning.

A popular morning prayer from *A Course in Miracles* suggest that we ask for inspiration by asking the divine: "What would you have me do? Where would you have me go? What would you have me do? What would you have me say, and to whom?" The idea is that you only act on true inspiration, not ego-based instruction.

I never intended to shift the focus of my life to empowering others to liberate and love their Authentic Self, but this sense of purpose and meaning is much bigger than me. Aligning my life purpose with my innate strengths and passions has allowed me to craft a life and lifestyle that provides continuous growth, fulfillment and joy.

Once I shared my personal experience with depression, anxiety and lack of self-love on a global platform, I found a deep desire to help more people break free from the prison of self-loathing. I heard from troubled souls around the world, male and female, young and old, in school and well into unfulfilling careers who sent me messages asking for help. And suddenly my life took on new meaning and purpose.

7

Architect Your Diamond Life

Now that you've reclaimed responsibility for architecting your life, you can utilize your personal power to set yourself up to enjoy the feelings and experiences you desire most. Armed with you Paradigms of Possibility from Part 1, and by accessing your spiritual passion you will now align your life journey with your values, strengths, dreams and inspiration to create an epic life based on your wishes for fulfillment, meaning, purpose and joy.

This is precisely what I did after coming to realize that I have the sole privilege of designing my life. I deliberately set out to put myself in situations and environments where I could openly explore my true desires, fully utilize my talents, and optimally express my passions. Reclaiming authority for my life and my experiences set me on a path to really living with vitality, passion, and purpose — three key elements and values I define as important for me.

Over the years I've come to know many people who are doing the same. To get to this point of power and purpose I personally use and teach my clients a system called Diamond Life Design, which was created by my friend Deri Llewellyn-Davies. It provides a comprehensive framework for designing your entire life in alignment with heart and soul.

Deri is someone who has deliberately created a life that looks like an epic movie. From running multiple successful businesses, advising entrepreneurs, speaking on stages around the world, to being a fully present father of three beautiful daughters, he seems to be living a diamond life. When you add into the mix his Global Grand Slam Adventure plan, which is filled with a variety of bold exploits such as climbing the highest peak on each of the seven continents, completing an Iron Man competition, running the Marathon des Sables, and more, you'll be amazed and inspired. You can read about his intense, excitement-filled life in his first book, *Life's Great* Adventure. Deri also he shared a recent death-defying story from Mount Everest in my book *Time to Rise.*

When I asked Deri years ago how he's managed to find the time and energy to do all that he does, he told me about his Diamond Life Design system and it struck me how well aligned it is with my approach to lifestyle planning. Deri's methodical approach to personal development and life enhancement was never something he thought he'd bring to the masses, but I convinced him that this system could help millions of people improve their lives. Then we decided to partner up to get the system out to a global audience. You have access to a free online masterclass where Deri and I explain how to use the Diamond Life Design system to create your epic life. Just visit www.DiamondLifeDesign.com to download the Diamond framework and watch the free videos we've prepared for you.

I'll now take you through some of the essential elements in the rest of this chapter so that you, too, can create your own Diamond Life.

So many of us admit that we seek fulfillment of our feelings elsewhere, rather than from our own actions and mindset. As you take responsibility for your life you become infinitely more capable of creating a life that brings you the emotional, spiritual, and financial fulfillment you desire.

Identify the feelings you wish to experience

As we consider what sort of life you want to live, I invite you to look at the types of feelings you want to experience. It starts with making a conscious decision to really get clear on defining how you want to feel.

Whether there was neglect, abuse or moving from house to house several times, as children we have plenty of opportunities to feel that we are to blame for bad things happening or that we are less than perfect. Many of us didn't grow up feeling perfectly accepted or totally loved, even when our parents tried their best. That often sets us up for a lifetime of compensating for that lack by searching for positive feelings and emotions outside of ourselves. For some people, food provides loving comfort, and for others sex, drugs, shopping, relationship hopping, or gambling provide relief from the emotional pain deep within.

Eventually we recognize that none of those make us feel whole, loved, and fulfilled. So, we either keep searching or we take a good long look at ourselves and dig deep to contact the love inside. The good news is that we can generate positive emotion for ourselves without the negative side of effects of any temporary fix.

Take a look at the Diamond Life Design framework below. Positioned at the top and bottom of the Diamond are feelings — the ultimate feelings we wish to enjoy in life and those we ultimately seek in the moment to moment experience of every day.

To kick things off, answer me this: how are you feeling right now? This question rolls off the tongue in so many situations and often the response we give is basic, boring, and inauthentic. For example, how many times have you replied, "Fine" when asked this question yet you were feeling anything but?

No one really feels fine. If we're honest, most of us would say that we're stressed, overwhelmed, frustrated, or scared. Some of us are afraid to admit that we feel bad because of how others might judge us. But as you learned in the last chapter, you must be honest with yourself so you can identify what needs changing. Finding out how you feel *now* can help you better describe the feelings you want to feel in life.

So, if you could wake up with the most positive feelings imaginable, what would they be? What are the ultimate feelings and emotions you want to experience as you go through your day and week and months of the entire year?

And please, don't just say, "*Oh, I just want to be happy.*" Why not? Because it's not specific, or reproducible.

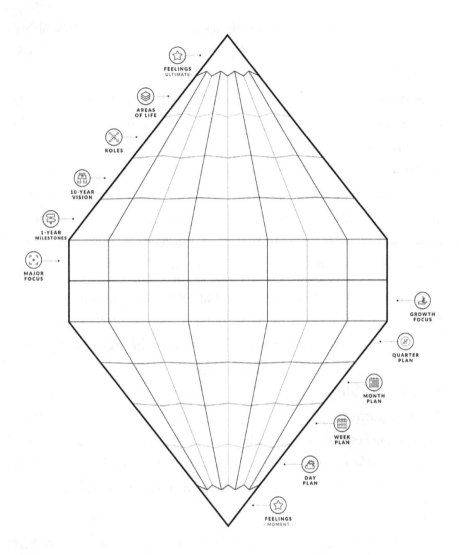

FEELINGS
· ULTIMATE ·

AREAS
OF LIFE

ROLES

10-YEAR
VISION

1-YEAR
MILESTONES

MAJOR
FOCUS

GROWTH
FOCUS

QUARTER
PLAN

MONTH
PLAN

WEEK
PLAN

DAY
PLAN

FEELINGS
· MOMENT ·

Look at the future vision you created in the last chapter and take a moment to dream a bit, to visualize, and to imagine your ideal life. Based on that vision write down all of the feelings you want to feel or experience — from bliss, to fulfillment, to excitement, to creativity, to passion.

Feelings are usually a momentary phenomenon. They show up in a moment and disappear the next. You'll notice as you look at the Diamond that we'll come back to feelings in every moment. This means you don't put off feeling great and expressing deep emotion some magical day in the far-off future. Instead, you'll deliberately set yourself up to experience those feelings and emotions, recognizing them as fuel for motivation and manifestation. On a regular basis you'll be prompted to ask yourself, "how do I create these feelings right now?" The good news is that you can optimize your life to create the cause and conditions for more of those moments *now*.

As you move down on the Diamond, into the areas of life, you're going to reflect and ask, *"What do I want to feel in this area of life."* The words I choose will likely be totally different from yours, so be sure to tune into your own heart to find words that really describe the life you want. For me, it is about bliss, purpose, and deep fulfillment. So, I set my life up to produce moments where bliss comes easily — through meditation, spiritual practice, and creative self-expression. I choose my professional projects and work to align with my purpose in life and those that will produce deep fulfillment.

Deri explained to me that bliss is a feeling he seeks, too, but he gets his dose of bliss in a different way, on mountains or while standing in the middle of nature. He says that being surrounded by Mother Nature produces bliss for him.

One reason I like the structure of the Diamond laid out this way is that over time it has prompted me to consciously look at certain areas of my life where I was feeling bad. And whether that bad feeling was depression, anger, or frustration what I did was to simply come back to my center and ask again, "What do I really want to feel?"

This made it easier to pinpoint the things that needed addressing. It was also easier to identify what was causing the frustration or bad feeling. I could tell when a situation had to change, or if people had to be removed from my life, or if I had to change myself, leave a situation, relationship, job, or country. I took control by looking deeply into the situation and myself to see what change I needed to create so I could bring back the ultimate feelings I desired.

For me, *feelings are my compass.* As you learned in Chapter 5 *our feelings are messengers.* They can tell us when we're a little bit off track or off course from our desired destination or state of being. So, I highly suggest you start here. You'll find that your feelings rarely steer you in the wrong direction. Your ego might, however.

For example, some people have asked Deri about his Everest expeditions. And many people exclaim, "I want to climb Everest, too!" But when you dig deeper to understand the feeling underlying that comment, you may find that it's ego based, meaning the ego wants some sort of validation, recognition, or approval. The difference, says Deri, is that setting up life goals for egoic achievement may not produce the lasting feeling you desire.

On the other hand, my friend, Missy Crutchfield, Co-founder of the Gandhi Global Center for Peace, also has a desire to revisit Mount Everest. She says that a calling from the mountain, from Mother Gaia herself, has inspired her to return to Everest to experience it more deeply. Aligned with her soul's desire, she has decided join me and Deri there for a spiritual visit to holy sites of Tibet in the coming years. Missy is dialed into the feelings that drive her work of activism and they guide her daily. (You can learn about and join the spiritual retreats we lead around the world at www.DiamondLifeDesign.com)

Once again, I ask you to honestly answer the question: how are you feeling now? And how do you really want to feel? This will lead you to find the activities in life which will deliver you opportunities to feel them.

Another inspiring reminder about feelings comes from Gregg Braden. In his book *The Lost Mode of Prayer* he describes an ancient practice of prayer. Based on his research, he says that the "lost mode" is a prayer that's based solely in feeling. Rather than the sense of helplessness that often leads us to ask for assistance from a higher power, feeling-based prayer acknowledges our ability to communicate with the intelligent force that 95 percent of us believe in, and we can participate in the outcome.

This mode of prayer simply invites us to feel a clear and powerful feeling as if our prayers have already been answered. Through this intangible "language," we can manifest our deepest desires. Gregg says we are always feeling in each moment of every day of our lives. While we may not always be aware of just what we're feeling, we are feeling nonetheless. If feeling is the prayer and we're always feeling, then that means we're always in a state of prayer. Each moment is a prayer. Life is a prayer!

Now that you have taken responsibility for your life and since you're always sending a message out to the universe, it is wise to beam out the feelings you really want to see mirrored back to you.

"Life" is the Mind of God sending back to us what we feel —
what we've prayed.

Explore the dark side of your feelings

For so long I was ashamed when I felt what I considered negative emotions. I thought that because I am actively living my spiritual path, I was never supposed to feel anger. Others might think they should never feel jealous or envious. But we have to acknowledge all of our feelings, including the ones that you might deem negative, so you can go beyond them and understand where they came from. That is how you can get dialed into a direction or set forth on a path to bring you the positive version of that emotion.

If there are feelings of uncertainty, fear, or frustration present now, write those down and then think about the emotions that would be their opposites. If you do feel like crap right now, if you're in a low place, I get it. Depression is common these days. Deri and I both admit how we've both experienced lows when our entire self-worth was tied to wealth or status. We're both able to speak to that issue. And if you're there, it's not likely you're instantly going to flip into pursuing a feeling of passion. You may just want to stop feeling like you do now. In that case start to look at what those feelings are like. For the moment, your only goal may be to feel a little bit better. And that's it. If that means you need to take a walk or have a nice meal, do that.

Keep practicing the Attunement Meditation or the other modalities described in the last chapter to release or transform those emotions — but only after you have taken note of their message to you.

Remember, this is a whole journey of life to be architected. Most negative emotions don't flip like switches unless there is a momentous event, like what I experienced in my near-death-like experience. In Deri's case, his conversation with his father just moments before he died was something that woke him up quickly. Check out his TED talk, F*** The Fear, It's Not Real Any Way, to hear him poignantly describe his experience of hearing his dad say how much regret he felt about the things he didn't do in life.

If you're feeling numb right now, or empty, or frustrated, whatever, don't ignore those feelings. They are warning signals. Instead, you should ask yourself, "What do I want to be feeling?" Make a list of the two to ten feelings that are most important to you and write them on your Diamond.

Write your ultimate feelings list

One of the major feelings I desire in life is passion. And when it comes to the roles I play in life, I want to feel passionate about everything I do. But how does that really look? For me you'll see passion come through as creativity, with my creative energy flowing; this is vitally important to me. I realize that's not a word that would be on everyone's list but in my experience, if I don't feel fully expressed I feel shut down or closed off. That will lead to depression if I let it stick around for long.

Love and connection are other feelings that I seek on a deep level. Connectedness, for me, is an honest heart-to-heart or soul-to-soul connection. This represents the deep intimate connection I have with close friends, and not just in a romantic relationship. The feeling of being genuinely, truly connected from the heart with people I love and admire is very important in my life. This is why my work, play and home life are all crafted to allow for rich, intimate connection.

Spiritual purpose also comes through everything I do. When I live according to my true nature and I feel like I am living my purpose, what some call pursuing my true dharma, it provides a positive feeling that governs everything in my life. I've had periods in my life when I was chasing the next project, achievement, or shiny business opportunity that came along, whether for money, recognition or just novelty. Being a multi-passionate entrepreneurial creative, this is a frequent challenge!

So, if I notice that I've gone too far off on a tangent in my business life, I recognize it quicker now. Then I ask, "Am I serving the business or am I serving my dharma? Am I working in alignment with my spiritual purpose?" If I don't feel like I'm on purpose, then I'm endlessly spinning on that hamster wheel, which ultimately blocks my fulfillment. And when I don't feel that sense of fulfillment and I don't feel that I'm on purpose then I know I'm at risk for a breakdown or a breakup.

As you write down your ultimate desired feelings, choose the words that are right for you bearing in mind that ultimate feelings may change. Just think about the words that resonate with you *now*. The words you choose will constantly reaffirm what you really seek. Equally, they become your guiding light. As you look at particular areas of life, such as money or abundance, what are the feelings you want to experience there? This may be totally different from the standard money affirmations people toss around. Based on your upbringing or past experience, you may find that safety is important. Feeling safe, secure, and certain could be crucial.

As you think about your work or business, what do you want to feel there? Most of us want to feel a sense of significance, that what we do truly matters. And certainly, we may want to feel proud. Because pride can be a double-edged sword, we must be conscious about how we express it and pursue it. If you're looking for your work to make you seem like a valuable person, pause and go deeper. You're already valuable, just as you are.

It's true the work you do and the contribution you make to others can be significant and it can make you feel proud for a job well done. Seeing and knowing you've shifted someone's life or business for the better can instill you with a sense of healthy pride, nothing wrong with that at all. You will naturally experience these emotions if you've done something aligned with your values. And that's the important thing.

As you think about your body, your relationships, and your home life, identify the most important feelings and emotions you desire. Add them to your list of the feelings you ultimately desire to experience. If you print out the Diamond Life diagram they can float above the point of the Diamond, almost shining like a beacon and you come to regard them as your guiding lights.

To be certain that your three flow centers are truly aligned with the feelings you select to put at the top of your Diamond you can repeat the EAM release statement to clear any resistance and then repeat the positive affirming statement. This will put you in the best position to welcome in opportunities, to receive and experience those emotions.

Define your areas of life

For most people there are familiar parts of all of our lives that deserve ongoing attention and focus. If you're familiar with the Wheel of Life planning system, then you may already have an idea of which ones are relevant to you. Rather than being prescriptive and laying out 8 specific areas to rate yourself on, the Diamond Life Design system is meant to give you the freedom to choose your areas — whether 6, 8 or 10 — and you name them in ways that are most inspiring and meaningful to you.

Look at your own life and consider which of the following need to be focused on when planning your ultimate life. Here's a list to choose from:

- Physical health

- Emotional well-being

- Home and garden

- Relationships (including family, friends, and intimate love relationships)

- Finances, wealth or abundance

- Business or career

- Hobbies or leisure activities

- Education or your own personal growth and development

- Your spiritual life

- Travel, adventure, and exploration

- Community service, philanthropy, charity

Based on the areas of your life that require or deserve your attention and planning, what would you call them? You can stick with the labels I've listed, but you may find it helpful to rename them based on the energy or inspiration you want to invoke in yourself when you consider them.

For example, physical health translates to Ageless Vitality on my Diamond. This takes into account my desire to feel vibrant energy year after year, full of youthful vigor no matter my age. Most people don't think about the quality of life they want as they age. In fact, most people think they can focus on health later, and instead drive themselves into the ground hustling, working, or partying. When you think of your health, are there specific illnesses you should be mindful of now, based on your family history? Is your weight steadily increasing year by year? Are you proactively considering your longevity, immunity, and resistance to mental decline?

When you really get honest and open about your responsibility to care for, nurture, and protect your body, you can then orchestrate your whole life to support you.

How about relationships? You could separate each of your relationship areas if they need special attention. For me, my life as a mom requires that I plan special time with my daughter to travel and be fully present as she enters her teenage years. So, this area corresponds to my role as Mother, which you'll see in the next section. In this area of my life I am mindful of my desire to feel present and deeply connected (from my Ultimate Feelings list).

If you're not married or in a relationship, you may choose to carve out that area so you can put your energy and intention into manifesting the healthy relationship you desire. You'll see as we move down the Diamond we'll get very specific with clear goals and milestones we need to plan for in order to feel totally fulfilled in each area. So, give the areas of greatest importance which may require focus and planning, their own section.

If you know that you tend to neglect planning for major vacations or trips, you may decide it is time to put Travel as a priority area of life. Likewise, if you've been flying by the seat of your pants in terms of your money management or spending, perhaps this is a good time to get serious about building wealth, or getting out of debt. A lot of people will call this area of life "money." Call it what you feel is right. I call it Abundance. This implies to me that there is always more than enough. Deri calls it Abundance Flowing Naturally. He likes to have the energy of flow in the label because he generously gives his money and resources to a variety of charities and organizations. This gives him a sense of fulfillment and purpose in life.

The topic of money can come across as dry, especially since so many people have very negative associations with money. For those who grew up in a family facing financial troubles, with parents who may made excuses for the lack by saying that "money is the root of all evil," or that "rich people are selfish," it can be hard for you to get excited to make and keep money. If that's true, then consider doing some of the clearing work we described in the last chapter.

Money is really about energy. It gives us an easy way to make an exchange of value between people or companies. This is a very healthy way to look at it. In my eyes, money is fabulous and can be used for the greater good. I see money as an enabler. I'm here to do good work while I'm alive and money makes that easier.

As for the idea of abundant flow, I like Deri's description because we don't aim to get money merely for the sake of acquiring stuff or piling it up in a bank. For me, it's about flow because when we are filled to overflowing, we then have more to give, and it keeps coming in. It's always flowing and there is no lack.

Money, whether we like it or not, is a huge part of life. It's the biggest part of business, and one of the biggest stressors. So, if we're going to free ourselves up across all areas of life and architect our lives fully, we have to embrace this concept of abundance around money. I work with a lot of healers, therapists, and spiritual Lightworkers. And when I hear that phrase, "Oh, it's not about the money... It's not about the profit," I get curious. Because the reality is, if we have a really amazing idea for a charity or for a healing practice, we need to have that abundance flowing for the greater good so that we can help those who are truly in need. So maybe there's a middle ground you can get to. Just don't hide from it. You just have to recognize where it fits and how it serves you in the larger architecture of life.

List the roles you play

As you look at the various roles that you play in each of the areas of life, you also refer back to feelings. What are the feelings these roles should give me? As we become more conscious as the architects of our lives, we may notice that we're playing some roles in life that we don't want to play. Or we may see when we are spending too much time in some roles which are not fulfilling and not enough time in roles that could really light us up.

Deri told me about one of the very important areas of life for him, which he calls Travel and Adventure. In that role he travels to visit the various wonders of the world. And one of his special roles in this area is 'Creator of magic moments.' Isn't that beautiful? The wording alone evokes a certain energy and emotion.

It would be very easy for Deri to just label himself a traveler or adventurer. But what brings him the sense of enjoyment and fulfillment is the magic he experiences on his adventures. In everyday life he could feel a big void since he cannot travel on major expeditions every week or even every month. So, he found that what he wanted was to create magic moments, for himself, for his kids and ultimately for his loved one.

Deri shared how he recently loaded his daughters into the back of the car and off they went for an adventure. He parked in a random place they'd never been to before and we walked around. They ended up on the Wye river where they cracked open a picnic. They sat on the riverbank skimming stones and enjoyed the picnic. They took a family selfie to capture their magic moment. That's how you can bring the big, ultimate feelings that you want to experience in life into the present moment on a smaller scale in daily life.

While it's very easy for us to enumerate the various roles that we play as mother, wife, daughter, CEO, author, etc., be sure to add an element of inspiration and magic to add a new dimension to your life. I am an international speaker. I am an author. All of these are different roles and each of these need different commitments, different dedication of time and attention.

I have also deliberately created a role as 'Coach' for myself. While I have mentors in my spiritual and business life, I also rely on myself as my own coach. I have realized that part of good self-nurturing and self-care requires that I give space and attention to my own development and encouragement. As my own coach I pay attention to what I need to feel whole, balanced and happy. Music is one element that I can rely on to energize me or relax me. If I suddenly no longer had music in my life it would not be pretty. Like all of the other things that are fundamental to me such as excellent plant-based nutrition, adequate sleep and alone time, if music is missing I feel off balance. If something tough is going on in my life and I'm feeling low, whether that's an energy low or a mood low, I always know I can just change the soundtrack to my life. Changing the music changes my energy and my mood.

So, consider the various roles you play already, and if you also need to become a mindful Coach to yourself, add that in.

As we continue to work with the Diamond Life Design system, you'll start to see these roles are architected in different areas. With certain roles like a son or daughter, these are not something we are actively doing every day for most of us. But if we don't actively give them attention our family dynamics will fall apart. Since moving to France with my daughter, I've made checking in with my parents back in the USA a regular occurrence, for example.

Every area of life brings a different rhythm. And every role of life brings a different rhythm. And if we don't understand and architect in harmony with those rhythms, we can very easily build a role in life in which we'll experience a lot of regret. We just need to consciously consider them. Once it's done, it's quite elegant. It's quite easy. And lso when you're out of flow, you come check back in on your Diamond and you can find what needs adjusting to get you back in flow.

Next up is the part of the Diamond that inspires me the most!

Describe your 10-year vision

I love this part because it's when we can dream really big. That's because we start with the 10-year vision. So many people get scared of dreaming big. But if you don't dream big, the actions you're taking day to day are never going to lead you to anything big. So beyond creating a vision board, this is not about wishing and hoping with, "One day I'll be there." By first describing a 10-year, then a yearly vision, we'll be forced to bring it right back home by asking, "what are you going to do about it now?"

I encourage you to look at *who* you are and *where* you are today and get really bold by creating a "stretch goal." That is, a goal that will require you to stretch, grow, or extend yourself massively to reach it. This is going to help you break out of the sticky hold of mediocrity and start orchestrating a truly epic life.

Because I don't do well with regret (it's the one feeling in the human realm that drives me bananas), I make sure that my 10-year vision is one that inspires me to look to my future with enthusiasm and optimism. On the flip side, if I look over the last ten years of my life and examine the things that I've regretted not doing, or not improving, or not exploring, this informs a lot of what I design for the future.

Being brutally honest about the excuses, laziness, or lack of focus that has caused me to regret my choices, I get really punchy and proactive to avoid regret at all costs. This stance has allowed me to say, "Okay, if I'm really badass and bold, what would I envision for the next ten years such that getting there, I won't have feelings of regret"?

I choose to create a vision based on the idea that I'll be living as my most bold, Authentic Self, expressing my talents and passions in the most outgoing and fulfilling way, and having the impact I truly desire. This doesn't necessarily mean I'll have achieved all of it, but at least I would've put it in place and started implementing a plan to avoid that feeling of regret.

If you consciously think about it, a lot of people just go through life muddling along. Then, as some get into a midlife crisis they realize it's because they haven't architected properly. Since I am in my forties, I do have enough experience (and wisdom hopefully!) to look back on the mistakes of the last few decades, but also to see where my strengths really lie. This shows me what has served me to create success.

And since I'm a visionary, when I go into my meditations, I visualize how I'll look and feel when I am at that 10-year vision. I consider where I am: Am I on stage? Am I lying on a beach? Am I alone, or with my beloved?

When you print out the Diamond you could utilize some pictures and use it as a vision board. Put the pictures of the 10-year vision up. You'll then have a massive blueprint of how to get that vision started. Next to it write a phrase or a few words that tell you exactly what the vision means for you and the feeling associated with it. Remember, if the feeling is not there, you have the wrong vision.

Outline your 1-year milestones

Now you've done the big work. This is where a lot of people who create a vision board leave it, and ultimately where the vision process ends. But my friend, we have to bring it home in practical terms now, or nothing is going to happen. In order to make progress each year we should move closer and closer to that 10-year vision. And there are likely to be predictable steps or milestones you'll see along the journey.

This step gives you something concrete to focus on and to motivate yourself. This is where the architecture really begins. So, you know the feelings you want to experience in each of your areas of life, you've defined your roles and described a juicy vision. Now we take each component, one by one, and answer the question: "What's this year's focus all about? What activities or achievements in the next twelve months are going to add up over time to get me to my 10-year vision?"

You might create specific goals for the year like earning a particular amount of money. Or setting up your business, or getting your career to the next level. If you wanted to become the world's greatest speaker in ten years, then you'll likely want to start speaking this year. If you know you want to master a skill, buy a new home, travel to exotic places, you've got to lay out the steps to get there, starting now.

This is where it gets sort of like basic goal setting, but this is across the whole of life. And as we talked about in Chapter 4, having specific timelines and milestones gives you a target for your accountability practice. You'll see that the lower part of the Diamond takes you into the element you need to focus on for your growth. If your 10-year vision was imagined sufficiently grand, it will require that you grow. Becoming deliberate and mindful of how you architect your life so you continue to evolve and develop is built into this beautiful system.

You can see that you are called to develop a quarter, month, week, and day plan, which requires you to be deliberate in your set up. This is why we don't put fluffy stuff up on a vision board and think it will magically manifest for us. So many people have tried that approach and end up frustrated, disappointed, then they give up on their dreams.

To live an extraordinary life is going to take focus and likely some years of work. You've got to be dedicated year after year in taking the steps that lead to progress.

The really beautiful part of this system is that at a glance, you'll start to see the flaws in your Diamond. It's going to start to become clearer and clearer as you go down the Diamond, you may discover where you are lacking in attention or details. Or you'll notice that you're overloaded in one area and light in another.

You may see that you're smashing it in the business area, but you're smashing it *too much* and haven't left sufficient time or energy to be present for your family. You might have the money bit sorted. You might even have the health bit sorted as well. But you may not have prioritized how you want to connect with yourself or your soul. It's a good thing to see the flaws, since it's an important first step to fixing them.

These are the basic principles of the Diamond Life Design framework. It is the logical next step you'll take in living as your Authentic Self. Once again, I invite you to watch the Masterclass that Deri and I did on how to use this framework to architect your Diamond Life. You can see each of us goes through every layer of the Diamond, so you have ultimate clarity and guidance. Visit www.DiamondLifeDesign.com for access to the Masterclass and if you'd like additional guidance and support, you can join our membership program.

The Cornerstone Process
Step 5 — Appreciation

How can I appreciate what life offers while I'm still living everyday life?

In the fifth and final step, Appreciation, your Cornerstone Process is complete. Here we dive further into the rich world of positive psychology, with techniques for appreciating the good that is inherent in your life. Beauty, altruism, awe, and humor can all be found in every life situation and you play a major role in generating them. When you experience your direct connection to the things in life worth appreciating, you'll not only enjoy the direct physical benefits such as increased happiness, lower stress, better sleep, and more intimacy but also a greater satisfaction for life and your indispensable role in it!

Here we watch with joy as our personal transformation runs its course. As life brings change and enlightenment to you, it becomes clear that *NOW* is the time to fully appreciate what IS — without attachment.

You'll now learn the value of charting your progress to see how powerful you really are, and to recognize the small steps and big leaps you make along your journey. You're invited to commit to celebrating your success and spreading your joy to others. We start by practicing gratitude.

Practice Gratitude

Positive psychology studies show that the practice of gratitude also creates a deep sense of appreciation for what one already has in life. Too often we don't realize how much abundance we live with every day. Within us is an abundance of ideas, creativity, beauty, and love. By practicing gratitude for who we are and what we have, we can also increase our sense of self-worth.

As you look at your life, can you find moments where you witnessed or expressed strength, beauty, or compassion? Can you identify times when you were really loving, empathetic, or helpful? How about times when you've been successful or accomplished something important to you? What about times when others praised you for something you thought was simple or natural? Have you endured a challenge or been brave in the face of something scary?

There are certainly admirable qualities in you, so find elements of your life, your personality, or your character traits, that are worth appreciating and write them down in your journal. Though we can always evolve and grow, it's helpful to acknowledge and appreciate what we have, the good within us now, and shower gratitude on ourselves. Recognizing the good in you also builds confidence. Similarly, you can be appreciative of the loving people in your life, your partners, even the ones who are no longer in your life. Practice opening your mind and heart with gratitude and appreciation and be uplifted by the positive mental energy.

Continue the practice you started in Chapter 3, each day, whether at night before going to sleep or first thing in the morning before getting out of bed. Write down three to five things that you are grateful for. They can be simple and mundane or deeply inspiring and profound. It makes no difference because the science behind the practice shows it will help you bring forth more joy and positivity. Appreciation for life will sink into your psyche and your brain, regardless.

Write at least a sentence for each thing you're grateful for to put your body and eyes into motion, causing the gratitude to go deep into your whole being. If you can add some sensory elements to each one, you'll activate even more of your brain to register the goodness in what you're writing about. This will help your brain take note of more of these things in the world around you — setting you up for more of that goodness to come into your field of view.

Don't fall into a pattern of always writing the same thing each day. You don't want to become desensitized to the goodness of your life. So even if every day you truly are grateful for your family, work or home, describe new aspects that inspire appreciation.

Examples:

Today I am grateful...

- for the sun and the warmth I feel as the rays stream through the window

- that my daughter can now make her own breakfast and clean up after herself before school

- for my bravery to put this book out to the world

- the sweet love note my beloved put into my purse without my knowing it

- wifi in my favorite café (yep, even the little things count!)

Making appreciation a daily part of your life will ensure that you focus on the most important parts of life and keep making magic.

Conclusion

The principles in this book have truly become a way of life for me, and I hope they do for you as well. Living the Cornerstone Process and designing my Diamond Life has kept depression at bay and given more meaning and purpose to my life. From **Awareness** of our positive qualities, natural personality, strengths and talents, to **Acceptance** of our basic goodness and right to happiness, it makes sense that we can become **Accountable** and responsible for our life. Asking our higher self, Source or the Divine for guidance on the most **Inspiring Action** to take can help us surrender our senseless striving and live with **Appreciation** for this precious human life. Then we can consciously create a vision for our lives that calls us to step up, evolve and express our greatest potential, in service to all of Life.

Please know that when I suggest that you keep your eyes on an inspiring vision, I am no different. Right now, I'm looking forward to my big 10-year vision and it truly inspires me. To be honest it scares me just a bit, too! As I prepare to celebrate my birthday in a few weeks I am taking time reflect on the past year and the last several years of my life. I've been playing full out, sharing my truth on stages and across the airwaves consistently for five solid years now. I'm humbled and inspired by the response I've received. I do not exaggerate when I say that it still surprises me and I'm feel privileged that I get to call this life mine.

This year marks nine years of living my Diamond Life on the French Riviera. I feel energized and full of vitality. My daughter is healthy, thriving, and launching inspiring projects of her own. I'm feeling such a blissful, peaceful, passion for my life that I live in near constant appreciation.

But don't think for a moment that I'm resting on my laurels! I am indeed pushing myself, extending beyond my comfort zone and looking for more ways to grow. One of the ways I do that is to be around people who inspire me; people who show me that there's even more to life than I currently realize. In every area of life, I'm surrounded by greatness, and people who are inspired to go further.

What is most striking is that my business has morphed into a festive celebration of talent, creativity, and light. I publish books, launch personal brands in the media, and host my own radio show. I have recently combined my extensive (nerdy) study of medical nutrition, positive psychology and neuroscience-inspired biohacking and launched a holistic media platform, **In8Vitality**, blending ancient wisdom and modern science for enhanced vitality and life mastery. By the end of this year we will be offering neuro-feedback training to demonstrate to people how they can truly become masters of their life force energy — with evidence based on brain wave and heart rate monitoring!

I have also joined networks of inspirational people around the world who offer sacred retreats, workshops, and seminars that are deeply transformational. My time is spent doing what I love with an incredible group of healers, light workers, motivational speakers, and transformational leaders. This is why I highly recommend that you connect with a community, or work with colleagues who inspire you, too.

Being in the company of amazing people allows their special sauce to rub off on us, and if we let it, their magical qualities can also linger. Add in a few special rituals and deeply emotional experiences, and you've got a recipe for delicious transformational empowerment. So be on the lookout for opportunities to join in the fun with us. You'll meet many of these Joykeepers and wisdom holders, like Ofkje Teekens, Halina Goldstein, Helene Philipsen, Gitte Winter Graugaard and others, on my web platforms and shows.

Since I launched the first edition of this book, I have spent a lot of time with my friend and colleague, Sólveig Þórarinsdóttir. Sól, as she is called, is a true embodiment of what it means to embrace your Authentic Self while living, working and playing in harmony with your unique nature. Sól is living, breathing, and sharing the very same principles I've written about here in her own work, her personal life, and with her family.

When Sól invited me to spend time with her in Iceland this summer, I said YES! When I arrived in Keflavik Airport, I was buzzing with anticipation because of the energy I feel when in her presence. I knew I was in for a magical ride.

I met Sól in Spain a few years ago. It was a magical experience. While on stage sharing from my heart about my journey as a TV personality, speaker, and now mentor to Lightworkers. I explained my view of our emerging role in this present age of awakening, as more of us are inspired to embark upon a journey to becoming Global Luminaries.

I love interacting with my audience, especially when I present new information or new ways of thinking about our spiritual life and soul work. So, I was happy to hear people replying when I asked questions, and to see them nodding in agreement with my explanations, encouraged me. Including when I asked the crowd the question I asked you at the beginning of this book.

"If you strip away your title, ethnic background and even your gender, what is left? At your core, who are you? Who are you?"

I heard responses such as:

I am love.

I am soul.

I am God.

I am spirit.

I am one.

And from Sól I heard, "I am you."

To which I replied, "Yes, and I am you. You are me. I am you. So, if I am you and you are me, why would we ever be afraid to be boldly who we deeply desire to be? Why would we censor ourselves, judge ourselves, or judge others?"

As I moved on, I shared my story about how I had spent so many years judging myself, feeling like I was not good enough, not smart enough. I spoke of how hard I was on myself, with impossibly high standards of perfection that drove me to strive for achievement and approval. I was honest and vulnerable and fully present.

I managed to end on a high note and felt the energy of the crowd; they were appreciative and inspired. And indeed, speaking with these beautiful people over the next couple of days I learned that many of them also believed in the possibility of that future vision. Some, with tears in their eyes, thanked me for being so real, so open, and true to my mission. I was deeply touched.

In particular I was also moved to hear from Sól that she was deeply touched and moved to tears during my talk. She told me that my story was so closely related to her own that it was uncanny. Sól told me that she, too, wants to be able to stand on a global platform to share her truth, and her vision, for a world filled with love, so we agreed to keep in touch.

When I left Spain, I was curious to see who would take the messages of hope and inspiration and put them into action. I hugged many new friends with a commitment to return next year. I imagined that if the magic of our time together could be bottled and shared with the world with the same force of passion and unconditional love, we'd have a powerful force to share with the world. Was all of the talk mere fantasy and dreamy conjecture?

The short answer is no. Sól has done it. She has taken my teaching (and nudging!) and shared her new brand messages on radio and TV. She has been a cover story in magazines and newspapers, and she's completely transformed her business and claimed a bold mission, which she shared with poise and elegance on the TEDx stage in Peterborough.

And after visiting with her in Iceland the last two summers, I can truly say that I have been forever transformed. In each of my summer trips, Sól has created a magical atmosphere that encouraged me to go beyond my preconceived notions of who I was at the time. Through sacred ceremonies, soul nourishing cacao, sweat lodges, yoga and empowerment sessions I feel an up-leveling of my presence and my superpowers after being with her. She is a shaman with precious wisdom, patience and love to share with this world, and I can't help but take each meeting as an invitation to improve myself, and stretch beyond my limits.

One of the biggest transformations has been in my self-image. While I have been on the self-love train a long time and I feel deep acceptance for myself, I found that I previously thought of myself as too reserved, withdrawn and boring. Even with all of my empowered speech and inspired visions, I've previously said "I'm lame." Sound shocking? Yes, despite my preaching against the danger of negative self-talk, I would regularly claim that I was lame or boring. Pointing out the things I regularly avoided — like staying out late, or giving up of my need to be warm, and cozy — I admitted to being kind of a 'lame Mommy.' With my introverted nature as my excuse, I previously favored staying home on weekends, getting to bed early, turning down social invitations, and abstaining from outdoor activities in bad weather or in conditions that I couldn't control.

Lame. Lame. Lame.

I told you I'm not without my own flaws!

But thanks to Sól and her friends, I can honestly say, "I'm no longer lame!" The combined effects of attending bonfires by the sea, island hopping on speed boats and ferries, attending an outdoor concert 'past my bedtime', and singing in Icelandic 'til the wee hours of the morning, followed by intense hot yoga classes, a goddess circle during a full moon cacao ceremony, and a sweat lodge have pushed me completely outside of my comfort zone and my predetermined preferences.

I've discovered that I was living a somewhat dull life compared to what is possible if I would dare to try. I found that I had some limits I didn't even know existed. And then I blew right through them — with a bit of nudging and loving support from Sól.

And guess what? I surprised myself. I've discovered that I'm an amazing human being. This is not me boasting. This is an honest observation of the body and life form that my spirit is living in. I learned through Sól's example that I can exercise in the evening. (I previously refused to exercise in the afternoons or evenings claiming that my best energy was available during the morning.) Now I know that I can stay up late hanging out with beautiful people, even strangers and wake up the next day ready for another adventure. I can even be dripping with sweat and feel comfortable and even attractive that way. I got to bask in the glow and feel the radiance of an enlightened woman, a goddess truly aligned with her spiritual purpose, and fiercely burning with soul passion.

There was no way I was going to say no to the various experiences on offer. I admit, the idea of appearing "lame" to my Global Luminary mentee, made me step up my game a bit. How else could I justify my role as a leader into bold self-expression if I wasn't willing to experience and taste her way of being?

At every moment during my stay, I felt nurtured and supported; such is the uplifting presence of Sól. She radiates such confidence and self-assuredness that I felt the need to try some of that on myself. What I found was surprisingly comfortable, not fake. I was authentically being me, enjoying my own delicious goddess energy in the presence of other women who were also trying on their goddess style, and it was magical!

We laughed, we cried, we sang, and we drank in the luscious warmth of cacao with an openness to being transformed. And that is just what Sól intends to inspire millions of women (and men!) around the world to do.

Sól wants more people to crack open their hearts so they can experience more love for themselves, for their bodies, for their lives. I am committed to helping her achieve her mission of global expansion and widely sharing her Love Warrior mission. Sól is on fire with this mission because she has lived it personally. (You can read about her personal story of transformation in the chapter she wrote in a book I published called Time to Rise and check out some video interviews we did together on www.RealSelf.love)

I share this because you could look at me or someone like Sól and think that we have arrived at true self-love and therefore don't struggle anymore. But the reality is life is a journey of constant evolution and growth. And that inspires me.

As I flew home from Iceland, I was so damn proud of myself and so excited to take my newfound self-love to the next level. Knowing that there is even more I can be and bring forth totally charges me up! I'm bringing a renewed sense of purpose and openness to everything on my plate.

If you want to join me virtually — head over to my Facebook page and YouTube channel and turn notifications on. I'll be broadcasting live each week.

Much love,
Andrea

- Join me live on facebook.com/drandreapennington

- Subscribe to YouTube.com/PenningtonMedia

- Follow me on twitter.com/DrAndrea

- Check me out on Instagram.com/drandreapennington

About the Author

Dr. Andrea Pennington (@DrAndrea) is an integrative physician, acupuncturist, meditation teacher, and sex educator who has provided holistic health education to men and women for over seventeen years. She is also a bestselling author, international keynote and TEDx speaker, documentary filmmaker, and sought-after media personality.

Dr. Andrea's extensive study of medical nutrition, positive psychology and neuroscience-inspired biohacking led her to create a holistic media platform, **In8Vitality**, blending ancient wisdom and modern science for enhanced vitality and life mastery. And, as Founder of the **#RealSelfLove Movement**, Andrea speaks globally to reduce the stigma of mental illness and to support people on their journey to authentic living. Dr. Andrea has co-founded **Diamond Life Design** with her friend Deri Llewellyn-Davies to help people around the world take bold steps to consciously architect an epic life.

For nearly two decades, Dr. Andrea has shared her candid, empowering insights on vitality and resilience on the *Oprah Winfrey Show, the Dr. Oz Show*, iTV *This Morning*, CNN, the Today Show, LUXE-TV, Thrive Global and HuffingtonPost and as a news anchor for Discovery Health Channel. She also produced a four-part documentary series and DVD on Gaia-TV entitled *Simple Steps to a Balanced Natural Pregnancy*.

Dr. Andrea has appeared in several newspapers and magazines including Goop, Essence, Ebony, Newsweek, Soul & Spirit, Top Santé, The Sun, Red, and Stylist. She has also written or contributed to 10 books and her popular multimedia content experience, *The Orgasm Prescription for Women*, has been touted as one of the most comprehensive sexual and emotional health books of today.

Now as host of weekly live broadcasts on social media, she brings her insight and inspiration for purposeful living, conscious relationships and soulful success to a global audience. And as host of Sensual Vitality-TV, she brings her unique 'nerdy' blend of medical science, positive psychology, and mindfulness meditation, to empower women to show up authentically, love passionately, and live orgasmically.

Dr. Andrea is also a renowned personal brand architect, media producer, and communications specialist. Leveraging her 20+ years of experience in broadcast and digital media she proudly helps people bring their brilliance to the world through publishing and media production her **Global Luminary Academy** with **Make Your Mark Global Media**. Her popular **Stories with Soul LifeWriting & Storytelling workshop** is highly acclaimed among authors around the world and her **Speak from the Heart** & VIP **Speaker Circle** public speaking trainings are bestselling events for those who wish to share their message with impact around the world.

Dr. Andrea is also a highly acclaimed three-time international TEDx speaker, invited professor at the University of Monaco, and past mentor for the Global Institute for Extraordinary Women.

As shared in her inspiring TEDx talk entitled "Become Who You Really Are", Dr. Andrea explains that she started recovering from a long history of depression and anxiety when she learned to love and express her Authentic Self. Her second TEDx on mindfulness and meditation elaborates on how to create a stress-resistant personality with the top 10 traits of highly resilient people. And in her third TEDx she bared her soul and even dared to rock the mic with a live performance of her original song entitled, "I Love You, Me!"

Dr. Andrea is the creator of The Attunement MeditationTM, a 5-step mindfulness meditation taught online and used around the world to lower stress, boost resilience, and enhance sensuality, and orgasm capacity. Her popular 21-Day Compassion Meditation Series is also useful in breaking down barriers to self-love and deep intimacy.

Connect with Dr. Andrea online at:

www.AndreaPennington.com

www.RealSelf.love

www.DiamondLifeDesign.com

www.SensualVitality.tv and

www.MakeYourMarkGlobal.com

Get Social!

https://www.facebook.com/DrAndreaPennington

https://twitter.com/drandrea

https://www.linkedin.com/in/andreapennington

https://www.instagram.com/drandreapennington/

https://twitter.com/SVitalityTV

https://pinterest.com/sensualvitality/

https://www.instagram.com/sensualvitality/

Other Books Published by Make Your Mark Global

The Ultimate Self-help Book: How to Be Happy Confident & Stress Free, Change Your Life with Law Of Attraction & Energy Healing by Yvette Taylor

Magic and Miracles Created and Compiled by Andrea Pennington

Life After Trauma Created and Compiled by Andrea Pennington

The Magical Unfolding by Helen Rebello

The Orgasm Prescription for Women by Andrea Pennington

Time to Rise Created and Compiled by Andrea Pennington

SMILER Can Change it All by Gegga Birgis

The Book on Quantum Leaps for Leaders: The Practical Guide to Becoming a More Efficient and Effective Leader from the Inside Out by Bitta. R. Wiese

Turning Points Compiled and Edited by Andrea Pennington

How to Liberate and Love Your Authentic Self
by Andrea Pennington

The Top 10 Traits of Highly Resilient People
by Andrea Pennington

Daily Compassion Meditation: 21 Guided Meditations,
Quotes and Images to Inspire Love, Joy and Peace
by Andrea Pennington

Eat to Live: Protect Your Body + Brain + Beauty with Food
by Andrea Pennington

MAKE YOUR MARK GLOBAL

Get Published Share Your Message with the World

Make Your Mark Global is a branding, marketing and media agency based in the USA and French Riviera. We offer publishing, content development, and promotional services to heart-based, conscious authors who wish to have a lasting impact through the sharing and distribution of their transformative message. We also help authors build a strong online media presence and platform for greater visibility and provide speaker training.

If you'd like help writing, publishing, or promoting your book, or if you'd like to co-author a collaborative book, visit us online or call for a free consultation.

Visit www.MakeYourMarkGlobal.com or

Call +1 (707) 776-6310 or

Send an email to Andrea@MakeYourMarkGlobal.com

9 780999 494981